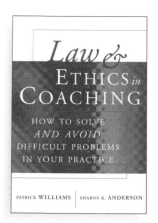

# THE SUCCESSFUL
# C O A C H

# THE SUCCESSFUL COACH

*Insider Secrets to Becoming a Top Coach*

Terri Levine
Larina Kase
Joe Vitale

WILEY

John Wiley & Sons, Inc.

*Library of Congress Cataloging-in-Publication Data:*

Levine, Terri.
   The successful coach : insider secrets to becoming a top coach / by Terri Levine, Larina Kase, and Joe Vitale.
      p.  cm.
  ISBN-13: 978-0-471-78996-3 (pbk.)
  ISBN-10: 0-471-78996-8 (pbk.)
  1. Personal coaching—Practice.  I. Kase, Larina.  II. Vitale, Joe, 1953–  III. Title.
  BF637.P36L485  2006
  158'.3—dc22                               2006003343

Printed in the United States of America.

10  9  8  7  6  5  4  3  2  1

# Contents

# Acknowledgments

I'd like to thank my husband, Mark, who gives me the space and freedom to be me and then fully loves me for who I am. Also my parents, Helen Levine and Walter Levine, who filled me high with self-esteem right from childhood, and all my amazing relatives (the Morgenbesser clan), especially my sister Lynn Boruchowitz, who seems to think I can do anything. My closest friends, Shannon and John Cane, Elaine Krinsky, and Betsy Lechner, who are always there for me. I'd also like to thank my mentors who taught me about business, marketing, and coaching, Eileen Seed, Thomas Leonard, Scott Hallman, Chet Holmes, Larry Loebig, and Sharon Teitelbaum.

To my wonderful business associates, Pat Zickefoose, Donna Eliassen, Sharon Wilson, Mary Heidkamp, Sue Guiher, Stefanie Hartman, Heather Lynn Jergens, Jan Carroll, and my nieces who work with me in my business, Sarah Lateer and Rachel Muraca, I simply could not accomplish any of what I do without you. You are all such superstars, and I am so appreciative of your creative talents (and what a treat to have my nieces working with me!).

I'd like to give huge thanks to my wonderful coauthors, Larina Kase and Joe Vitale. Joe has been one of my key mentors over the years and is a copywriting and marketing genius, and I feel honored to cocreate with him. Larina is an amazing woman, passionate and inspiring coach, and expert in knowing what the coaching market needs. These two fine people are a joy to play with.

Finally, I want to thank the Creator for giving each human being the power to create the life and work they desire and for the blessed life I am living.

# Introduction

In my "other life," I was a high-flying executive earning a ridiculously high salary. As far as everyone I knew was concerned, I had it all, yet I was deeply unhappy. I was working so hard that I didn't have a life. I was stressed. I was tired. On top of this, I felt terribly guilty. How dare I, a wealthy and successful career executive, complain when so many others out there had no jobs or worked equally as hard as I did for much less money. I felt very ungrateful, but I couldn't shake the feeling that this wasn't for me. Life wasn't meant to be this way, and one day I not only realized but also accepted that all that money I was earning meant nothing because it couldn't buy the one thing I wanted and needed most.

I hired a life coach, and through the coaching process discovered why I felt the way I did and what I wanted most to be doing. Life was ticking by, and I wanted and needed to experience more before it was too late. I wanted to achieve my dreams. My desire has always been to help others, and I was so enthralled and excited about my own coaching experience and knew how effective and right it was that I wanted to help others this way, too. Of course, it wasn't only the desire to switch careers that motivated this change. I wanted to work my own hours when it suited me, be my own boss—accountable to nobody else with all the freedom that entails—and I wanted to continue to earn good money. I wanted to earn my living doing something I loved. Well, doesn't everybody? Do we really want to get out of bed early in the morning and go and do something we hate and spend all day, and then some, doing it? Puh-leeze!

When I walked away from my six-figure income and said, "I am going into business for myself and I'll be working from home," people were shocked. My family and friends thought I had lost all my marbles and tried to talk me out of it, especially when they learned just what the business was that I was going into: coaching. You have to understand, in the early days of coaching, many thought it was just a fad and would soon pass. (I guess you could say I'm now having the last laugh!)

Everyone was convinced I was crazy and doomed to failure, poverty, and regrets. But this was my dream, and I had every right to pursue my dream, my way, in my life. I started in a coach-training program and got personal training from the coaching legend Thomas Leonard. I was very happy the day I sat and passed my examination, and when I began my new career, I attracted 30 clients in 15 days! And that was just the beginning!

I pushed myself beyond my limits and ventured far outside my comfort zone, discovering just how much I was capable of, and went on to attain the much-coveted master certified coach designation. But I didn't stop there! I stretched further, again amid cries of concern from well-meaning family and friends, and started my own coach-training program to teach others to become qualified, certified personal and business coaches. And I didn't stop there, either. I went on to found Comprehensive Coaching U, the coach training program for professionals, and the Coaching Institute, training life coaches around the world, and authored Amazon.com best seller *Work Yourself Happy*, which was followed by *Coaching for an Extraordinary Life, Create Your Ideal Body*, and another Amazon.com best seller, *Stop Managing, Start Coaching*. I also became a popular keynote and public speaker. I was, and still am, happier than a pig in mud! But I must tell you, I'm not naturally brave, yet look what I've achieved! You can do it, too!

And now, instead of being called crazy, I'm called other names. My clients have nicknamed me the "wisdom wizard," and a couple call me the "queen of coaching." What I do may be different, but it works! I am now privileged and honored to have the reputation of being known as one of the most successful coaches in the United States today, and I have attracted an international following that continues to delight me. My circle of friends, acquaintances, and associates widens with each passing month, and they live in places like the United Kingdom, Norway, Sweden, Denmark, Germany,

France, Turkey, Japan, Singapore, Australia, and New Zealand. This profession has truly blessed me in more ways than one!

And to think I may never have experienced this great joy in living! It took just one decision to hire my own coach, way back then, to turn my life around in ways I never dreamed would be possible.

Of course, it certainly helps that I have a background in business and marketing, and, yes, these skills certainly pushed me forward quickly when I was building my own coaching business. I left the corporate world with a track record of growing million-dollar businesses, so in many respects, I had a head start. And this is why my classes fill very quickly whenever I announce I am doing a marketing seminar. Naturally, other coaches want to know how I did it and continue to do it!

Nowadays, I am a nationally recognized authority on creating greater business and personal success, and I'm featured regularly in the media and on the Channel 10 NBC news in Philadelphia as a coaching expert. I still live in Pennsylvania, and when I'm not coaching, training, speaking, writing, or away on vacation, I *love* to race formula Dodge cars! (So okay, maybe I am still just a *little* crazy!)

And as to the question, why have I teamed up with Larina Kase and Joe Vitale to write this book? The answer is simple. The three of us have seen so many great coaches unable to make a great living as a coach or attract all the clients they wanted. We want *you* to enjoy what we're enjoying—success, happiness, freedom. You see, we know what it's like to yearn for something different but be too afraid to change and step into the unknown. We know how easily you can be a successful coach once you learn how and have expert coaches and mentors assisting you.

With this book, we hope to help you understand what is holding you back in your life! We want to help you identify the barriers and inner blocks stopping you from having the life you dream of, the freedom to do work you love and be paid for it. We want you to stop dreaming and start achieving!

To your success!

Terri Levine, CEO
The Coaching Institute

P.S. Visit me on my web site at http://www.TerriLevine.com.

xv

# PART 1

# Getting Ready to Become a Top Coach

# 1

# I Don't Know! Do I Want to Be a Coach or Something?

*Happy are those who dream dreams and are willing to pay the price to make them come true.*

— Anonymous

## "Coaching? It Sounds Great . . . but What Is It? Is It for Me?"

It's the fastest growing business in the world today. It's quite possible you've been toying with the idea of becoming a full- or part-time coach or consultant of some kind, or you've already completed your training and are daunted by the task of actually building a successful business. Or maybe you have already begun and want to know how to make business boom. Unlike other home-based businesses, this one is very rewarding, and we're not just talking about financially, although it certainly is that, too!

So, are you wondering if the coaching business is right for you? Unsure what it takes to start a coaching business? Then let's see if we can remove the mystery for you.

A coach, by Terri Levine's definition, is a person who is a guide and supports other people on their life and work journeys to create more of what they are wanting. That doesn't mean we give answers or advice, and it doesn't mean we teach or lead. It means we act as partners with our clients to discover what they want and how best to achieve it. It isn't about the coach having all the answers; it is about the coach helping the client tap into the answers.

Coaches aren't magical, and we aren't all necessarily brilliant. We simply have a drive to help others achieve more, and we have a strong desire to do this work.

The fact is, today, in most states, anyone can call themselves a coach. There are business coaches, wellness coaches, relationship coaches, life coaches, executive coaches, and fitness coaches. What sets coaches apart is their training and their specialty. So, before you make any decisions about if you should be a coach or whom you should coach or what training you need, let's help you find your passion and see if you are cut out for coaching. If you are, let's find out what's holding you back from becoming a top one.

## Check Your Passion

There is nothing more important in starting a new business than being sure *that* business is right for you and that you have a desire to be in that business. If you can't imagine being on the phone, or in person, with individuals or groups for much of the time, then this profession isn't a fit. If you get excited about speaking with people for most of the day and want to be self-employed, setting your own hours and your own fees, then coaching might be the right opportunity for you.

The most important thing is to be sure you feel a passion for doing this work. That you are so excited about the coaching business, owning your own business, and doing this work that you are willing to do the marketing (yes, marketing) that will allow you to share your passion with others.

If you can't see yourself being a coach and sharing the fact you are a coach with others, then you might be a great coach who never gets to work with clients. You must be willing either to do the marketing (or share your coaching passion with prospective clients) or to pay someone to do this for you. This doesn't mean that marketing has to be a dirty word or scary or manipulative. There are many resources to help you make this more fun—this book being one of those resources to help you.

## Proper Training

If you still feel you have the passion for coaching and a willingness to find fun, easy, effortless ways to market coaching, then keep going. Now it is time to find out how and where you can learn coaching skills and, most importantly, to understand how you learn. Some adults like to take home-study programs, others online courses, some prefer to read books, others do well with in-person training, some do well by mentoring, and others by telephone group classes. Get clear about how you prefer to learn.

To be an effective coach, you will need coach training by other experienced, successful coaches who provide your training using the method in which you learn best and who can help you select your coaching niche and areas of expertise.

You don't have to get your coach training in a standard way, nor do you have to belong to any coach lobbying organization or one of the various coaching associations or organizations to be an extraordinary coach.

You do need to have training that is fun, easy, and joyful for you, in which you really learn and can apply your learning, and in which you receive information and ideas that support you in your coaching business. Without the proper training, you will fall short of client expectations, you will have low self-confidence, and your chances of success will be much smaller.

Give yourself an advantage; find a training program to learn the skills you need. Do it for you and for your clients.

## What Coaches Do

We think it is very important for you to really see and feel what coaches do with their clients and what it is like to have a coaching business. We suggest to all new coaches that they speak with people doing coaching and get a feel for what they like about coaching, what their days are like, and what to expect. You wouldn't open a business without a clear picture, right?

When you have a vision for your coaching business, you will be able to achieve it. If you don't, your chances of succeeding are much lower. Having a clear vision for your coaching business is like driving a car with a crystal clear windshield. You probably remember a time when you drove along with a clear windshield and noticed all of the beautiful scenery and colors in the environment. Not having a vision is like driving with a dirty windshield; not only will it be less enjoyable, but you will be likely to wind up lost, take a wrong turn, or miss important signs. A great quote by Yogi Berra to illustrate this idea is: "If you don't know where you're going, you might wind up somewhere else."

When Terri received her master's degree in speech-language pathology many decades ago, she had no clear idea of what she was to do all day long in that profession. After spending lots of money, time, and energy to get that degree, she soon discovered that this profession was somewhat boring. Rather than you also discovering something like this later, do some research right now.

## Why Coaching Is Booming!

Coaching is a rapidly growing profession, both for personal coaches and professional coaches, because people are realizing, as are companies, that they need help. They have tried self-help books and tapes. They have brought consultants and trainers into their companies. But nothing has stuck, because once the book is read or the consultant leaves, we go back to our old ways.

The use of executive coaching is widely reported to be growing rapidly. A recent study published in Jeffrey E. Auerbach's *Seeing the Light: What Organizations Need to Know about Executive Coaching: The 2005 State of the Coaching Industry Report* provides hard data to show the increased utilization of executive coaching. The College of Executive Coaching and Jeffrey E. Auerbach surveyed 101 organizations, and 58 percent of respondents said coaching utilization increased in their organizations in the past year, and 95 percent said coaching increased in the past five years. None reported a decline in coaching utilization. This impressive finding suggests that organizations that have utilized coaching find it so valuable that they continually increase its usage, even though executive coaching can be an initially expensive service (Auerbach, 2005). Companies are getting a great return on their investment!

The reason this profession is one of the fastest-growing professions in the world is simple. Individuals and businesses have come to the same conclusion: They want help, and they want results that last. Coaching does this; the results last and the outcomes are measurable.

## Why Would People Hire *Me* to Coach Them?

Many coaches we have worked with ask why they would be hired. It is natural to wonder whether you will be truly successful and to doubt your own competencies. In this book, we will help you resolve some of the limiting beliefs about why people need to hire you.

So who gets hired? Coaches get hired because of their past experience in life and work and their skills and talents and because they have specialty coach training.

You will have clients hire you because of the jobs you've had, the education and experience you've had at work, what your values are, your natural skills, and the talents that you probably take for granted.

And, of course, they need to know about you to hire you. For this reason, we will dedicate several chapters to marketing your coaching business. Marketing works best when you build a niche around your own unique competencies and skills.

Terri knows a coach, a friend, whom she considers to be very organized. When this friend was looking for a coaching niche and deciding what types of clients to attract, Terri helped her see that one of the talents she took for granted—being organized—is in high demand and that many clients would hire a coach for this. She is now one of the top organizational coaches.

So, make a list of your life and work experiences. Go back, year by year, decade by decade. Where did you work? What are your skills, talents, abilities, and so forth? Where did you excel and shine?

## The Top Coaching Niches Now

You can be a coach in almost any specialty area and be successful. Of course, it is best to create a specific niche for yourself. These are the general niches that are thriving today:

1. **Health/wellness/weight-loss coaching.** Let's face it, the health industry and the weight-loss industry have been growing for years. With more people focused on self-care and alternative health practices, there is a huge demand for coaching in these areas. Larina Kase runs a program called STRENGTH Weight Loss & Wellness™ that certifies other professionals in weight-loss coaching (http://www.StrengthWeightLoss.com), and Terri has an extensive program at http://www.createyouridealbody.com.

2. **Sales coaching.** In the United States alone, there are more than 17 million people who sell. Coaches with this specialty are in demand and command top incomes. Learn more about this niche at http://www.bestsalescoachtraining.com.

3. **Career coaching.** This recession-proof niche is the largest coaching niche. When times are good, people change jobs or start their own businesses and hire career coaches. When things are tough and companies lay off people, people hire coaches to find a job or phase into a new career. Coaches in this niche will always be in demand. See more about this niche at http://www.terrilevine.com/workyourselfhappy.htm.

4. **Corporate and executive coaching.** Companies and their managers want to be more successful and want their businesses to make a profit. They also want their teams and leaders to possess more coaching skills. A recent article in the *Harvard Business Review* estimated that approximately $1 billion is spent annually on executive coaching in the United States (Sherman & Freas, 2004). Executive coaching is becoming prevalent in today's businesses, and there are excellent opportunities for executive coaches.

5. **Business coaching.** Small-business and entrepreneurship coaching are hot areas! There are dozens of specific niche areas, and you can choose a couple or even several within business coaching. Terri is a professional business coach who works with large corporate teams as well as individual entrepreneurs. To see how Terri and Larina integrate multiple niches within business coaching, see http://www.TerriLevine.com and http://www.PAScoaching.com.

6. **Personal coaching.** With all of us having more demands placed on our time and wondering about our life purpose, more people each year hire coaches to help them create better lives. Coaches working with individuals to get more out of life have many clients, as this is a very popular form of coaching. Learn more about this niche at http://www.coachinstitute.com/coachinginstituteorientation.htm.

7. **Parent coaching.** Family dynamics have changed. People are asking, "What's wrong with kids today?" Families are described as dysfunctional. Drug use, suicide, increased teenage pregnancies, school dropouts, runaways, crime, confusion—it's all here

and it's not a Hollywood movie. It's real. Children do not come with a guidebook, and what worked 10 to 20 years ago does not work today. Parents do not know what to do or how to cope, and with their busy lifestyles—and usually both parents work—they need ongoing support to learn and carry through new parenting skills designed for today's family! Learn more about this niche at http://www.certifiedparentcoach.com.

### *What the Best Coaches Have in Common*

The most successful and highly regarded coaches have the following skills and traits in common:

1. Can think on their feet.
2. Deep listening skills.
3. Ability to be with many kinds of people.
4. Nonjudgmental.
5. Ask powerful questions.
6. Make great observations.
7. Speak the truth.
8. Integrity.
9. Have a light perspective.
10. Excellent communication skills.

With approximately 25,000 coaches in the United States alone, coaching is an extremely popular field.

## Why Not Become a Top Coach?

We don't want you to be just any coach; we want you to become a top coach. When you are a top coach, you have an excellent platform for getting your ideas out to the public. You can help the most people, and you can enjoy a lucrative and rewarding career.

Coaches base their careers around helping others to achieve their goals. The problem is that many coaches do not know how to help themselves become the top in their fields. More than 50 percent of coaches are making less than $20,000 per year (Fairley & Stout, 2004).

Why? There are two reasons. The first is that coaches do not have information on how to build their businesses and market their services. There are dozens of excellent resources on this topic that tell coaches what they need to know to excel in their fields. We will highlight the most important marketing strategies for your coaching business.

For many coaches, the second reason is more salient: They are not putting into practice the knowledge about what works and how to succeed. You may know *what* you need to do to be successful: marketing, public speaking, writing, networking, and so on. But a problem occurs in translating this knowledge into action. Just as we know that we need to eat lower-calorie, healthful food and exercise to lose weight, we do not necessarily do it. Fears and self-doubts hold us back.

We've found that many people do not implement marketing ideas, or they do not do them as effectively as possible. Invariably, certain fears and insecurities come up and limit people from pursuing the marketing and sales tactics that will make their businesses take off.

Thousands of coaches and consultants suffer from fears and self-limiting beliefs about their credibility and competencies, their abilities to market their businesses, their internal motivation, and their likelihood of success. They engage in unhelpful behaviors, including procrastination, not using support effectively, and not setting the right goals.

## Meet Your Coaches

We are here to serve as your own success coaches. Our ideas will help you and your clients. No matter what type of coach you are, you can use the ideas in this book in your coaching, and your clients are sure to benefit. Together, we, Terri Levine, Larina Kase, and Joe Vitale, have helped hundreds of coaches and business owners, and now we're here to help you.

As the CEO of a coach-training program and an internationally recognized master coach herself, Terri will share her secrets of coaching success with you. For her, the proof is in the pudding: She has built and run several million-dollar companies and wants the same for you.

As a cognitive behavioral psychologist and business coach to professional service firms, Larina will help you overcome your limiting beliefs and master strategic marketing to help your business take off.

Joe will offer his expertise in personal development and market-ing. His insights are interspersed throughout. Every coach wants to know how Joe approaches Internet marketing. You may be sur-prised by what he says. (Hint, mastering Internet marketing is not as hard as you think.) Read Chapter 14 to find out.

In this book, we will help you learn what you need to know. In Part 1, we will help you overcome whatever holds you down so you can soar to the top. Even if one area does not sound like a problem for you, read it anyway. You may not be aware of difficulties in a particular topic until you read the chapters. Or you may learn some valuable ideas and techniques that can improve your coaching skills. This can help you help your clients overcome whatever holds you back and make your coaching extremely effective. Then, in Part 2, we'll give you many marketing tips and strategies to help you gain clients and build your business. Sound good? Keep reading.

# 2

# What's Stopping You from Being a Top Coach?

*I have not failed. I've just found 10,000 ways that don't work.*
—Thomas Alva Edison

In Part 2 of this book, we delve into the best marketing strategies to help your business succeed. Before we do that, we want to prepare you to really make these ideas work. You may wonder whether you'll be truly successful. You may wonder why your business is not yet extremely profitable. There are many things we do that hold us back. Are you ready to bring them out into the light and overcome them?

We'll present an overview to get you thinking about what might be holding you back. Start thinking about what might stop you from becoming a top coach. Read this chapter and begin thinking. We'll get into the details in later chapters.

## Mastering the Mind Game of Top Coaches

We often hold ourselves back professionally for the same reason we stop ourselves from jumping off a tall building. It is self-preservation. We think we are protecting ourselves, and sometimes we are, but it is the extent and lengths we go to that determine whether we go too far or not.

In coaching we speak a lot about *self-talk*. That is those small conversations you have inside your head that dissuade you from doing something. Many people engage in negative self-talk; you may be familiar with some of these conversations yourself:

- I couldn't do that.
- I'm not pretty/handsome enough.
- I'm so stupid!
- Why can't I ever do anything right?
- I'll never be rich!

These are examples of negative self-talk. Self-saboteurs are masters of negative self-talk. So, what's the problem with these conversations with yourself? You become what you think. What you might consider merely an offhand remark to yourself, when repeated often enough, becomes truth to your brain.

If you're putting off trying a career in coaching or consulting, maybe some of your negative self-talk might be:

- I'm not smart enough.
- I don't have enough money.
- I don't have enough time.
- I don't know anything about business.
- What if I invest all that time, energy, and money and I fail?

Would it surprise you to know that some successful entrepreneurs also have doubts? The difference between them and you is they have learned to feel the fear and do it anyway.

They've learned to replace their negative self-talk with positive self-talk:

- I can do that!
- You don't need to be Einstein to do that!
- I'm perfectly fine just the way I am!
- Where there's a will, there's a way, and I'm going to find it!

Feeling the fear and doing it anyway doesn't mean you take silly risks, but you do need to rationalize your fears and determine if what you're afraid of is real or not. A perceived danger is not a real danger. Whatever it is you fear, it may never happen! In fact, it probably won't happen! You just have too good an imagination. So why not use the power of your magnificent imagination more positively?

And when it comes to the crunch, what is fear anyway? It is just another emotion. If your thoughts can create fear, they can also dispel fear. Your self-talk can be your best ally in conquering your fears. If fear is blocking you from moving forward and experiencing more from life, starting your own business, or even scuba diving, analyze your fear. What is it you are really afraid of, and is it a rational fear? Fear of failure is a silly one because how do you know you're going to fail? You surely don't go into business with the plan to fail! Fear that you won't be able to cope is another silly one. You progress at your own pace. Nobody is forcing you to become an instant, overnight success! It rarely happens that way, in any case.

## Why Do Today What You Can Put Off until Tomorrow?

We've uncovered fear and negative self-talk; is there anything else?

Yes, a common one is procrastination. Does this scenario seem familiar to you? "Sure, I could check out coach training—all the major training schools have web sites. But actually, now is not really a good time because I have to clean out the garage!" Or how about, "I can do a business basics short course at night school. It wouldn't take long, but I work such long hours as it is. And it may only take a few months, but for me, it will feel like years! I'd fall asleep in class!" Or how about, "Maybe I could ring one of those coaching schools and ask about their home-study kits, because then I could study in my own time, when I'm feeling energetic. Well, I'll think about that after I've cleaned the attic!"

It's amazing how many of those awful jobs around the house get accomplished during these moments of procrastination. If your attic has waited 10 years to be cleaned out, don't you think it can wait another 10 minutes while you make a phone call? You're not signing your life away by finding out your options, and you never know, you just might be pleasantly surprised to find how easy it all can be for you.

Sometimes, there is more to procrastination than simply putting off doing something. Maybe your trouble is really that you are disorganized (and did you know you can hire a coach for that?). You can learn to prioritize the things you need to do each time and manage your time more effectively. If you really want or need to do something, the time is always available. We waste a lot of our spare time with frivolous activities or procrastination exercises. The real reason you procrastinate is to deliberately avoid doing something. And why do we avoid anything? Usually we are afraid!

So, you can go clean your attic if you choose, but if we had the choice, we'd rather make the 10-minute phone call. How can finding out about something be threatening? Are you afraid you'll discover you actually could afford coach training, and before you know it, you'll be giving up your secure job and coaching full time? And then are you thinking, "Will there be enough clients? What if I fail? What will I do then?"

How difficult is it to change that around and say to yourself, "I can have enough saved while I build my coaching practice," or "I can coach part-time while I build my practice, and that way I keep my day job and the security of a regular income," or "How great that I don't have large setup costs to be a coach—even I can afford it!"

And have you noticed the longer you put off doing something, the worse it becomes in your mind? Putting things off doesn't make them easier to tackle later; it makes them harder.

## Focused on Success

Of course, not all procrastination is caused by fear or avoidance issues. Sometimes, we have difficulty focusing on what we should be doing due to outside distractions. Some of these distractions can be unavoidable, such as young children in the house or unexpected visitors. It's when we allow these distractions to stop us from moving ahead that we get into trouble. We find it hard to get back into what we are doing when we are constantly distracted. The task becomes unnecessarily difficult. We develop a kind of fear of the task because we become confused and we are no longer sure of what we are doing and where we are. So what do we do in these instances? Well, some folks go clean the attic!

It is frustrating, yes, but not totally hopeless. What you need to do is manage your time more effectively. Tasks that require your focused attention should be scheduled at a time when children are either in school or in bed or can be looked after by your partner. Friends and family should be discouraged from visiting you during your official work hours if you are working from home. If you can't find 10 minutes to make a phone call to inquire about training, for example, then send an e-mail. You can send an e-mail or a letter at any time of the day or night, and it will still reach its destination. Saying you can't find 10 minutes of peace and quiet to make a phone call is just another excuse.

If you really want to be a coach or consultant and have the freedom of working your own hours and being your own boss, you need to focus your attention on one step at a time. Don't allow yourself to be overwhelmed by all the things you think you may need to do. Don't spread yourself too thin or you will be overwhelmed, those fears and doubts will raise their ugly heads, you will start with the negative self-talk, and before you know it, you'll be up cleaning the attic! And still no closer to attaining your dream!

Instead of letting imaginary fears rule your life, take control. Make the phone call, send the e-mail or write the letter, and find out what is involved in attaining your dream. Then you can look at things like finances, managing your time to fit it in, and prepare a business plan that will enable you to go after your dream in a way that feels good for you. Just take it one step at a time.

## Motivation Is Everything

Another reason you may be holding back from becoming a top coach is a lack of self-motivation. Some of us are born self-starters, and others need to be taught. Knowing that what you do is important, whether or not you receive outside recognition, is a key factor in being self-motivated. You become self-motivated when you enjoy the satisfaction of doing something well. You seek that. It makes you feel good about yourself. You also become self-motivated when you are passionate about something. High achievers are self-motivated by their need for either achievement or recognition or both.

*If you want to become a top coach or consultant you will need a healthy dose of self-motivation. You know what you need to do and should be doing, and it is up to you to see that you do it. Once you've started the doing, the fear drops away. Getting started in the first place seems to be where most people become stuck. Instead of being afraid of challenges, see them as exciting opportunities to test yourself and grow in new areas. Set your goals high but make them realistic—break them down into smaller goals. Be prepared to take a few calculated risks. Learn to appreciate the wonderful sense of achievement you will gain each time you reach a minigoal. Remember that none of today's superentrepreneurs were overnight successes, and it's true that everyone must start somewhere. (Start being the operative word here!)*

We're asking you to take a good look at yourself now and be honest:

- What motivates you? Once you have discovered that, use it to motivate yourself now.
- Do you have fears and doubts holding you back? Identify them. Are they realistic or imagined? Feel the fear and do it anyway. Life's too short, and you may never get a second chance.
- How are you sabotaging yourself? Do you procrastinate and deliberately avoid or put off doing things? What's the worst that could happen if you decided to just stop procrastinating one day and take an action step toward your dream?
- Do you have trouble focusing? Are you plagued by distractions? What can you do about these, and how can you best manage your time?

## Support for Your Success

Now you're thinking fear, lack of motivation, procrastination, and distractions are behind your self-sabotaging habit. Yes, that's quite true; however, there is more to it than that.

Not all, but some people experience blockages because:

- They don't believe they can do it on their own. They lack support.
- Modern technology frightens them, and they don't believe they can work with it, yet they believe they must work with it or be doomed to failure.
- They feel they really don't know enough themselves and fear that there are not enough sources of help or information available to help them.
- The thought of having to market themselves or their business terrifies them.

Let's look at these. First, you don't have to do it on your own. Many coaches partner and go into business in joint ventures, sharing expenses and the workload. Many coaches happily refer each other to potential new clients. Many of the larger, better-known coaching schools, such as the Coaching Institute, offer member forums where you can access information and advice 24–7. You don't have to be on your own! Or are you afraid your partner won't support your venture? Have you discussed it? It would be easier, of course, if your partner supports your business goals and is willing to help you achieve them, even if it is just to not disturb you between certain hours to enable you to focus! Not having your partner's support may make achieving your goal more challenging but not impossible.

Sometimes, the thought of being the boss can be overwhelming for some people. There is, after all, a modicum of comfort in knowing that if something goes wrong, the buck stops with somebody else, but when you are your own boss, it stops with you. You have total responsibility and control. This needn't be scary. There are plenty of resources available for coaches, so you need never feel that you are not equipped to handle any situation. The benefits of being your own boss far outweigh any possible disadvantages.

You do need to consider that some family members may very well consider your home business as a coach or consultant as nothing more than a hobby, albeit a very well-paid hobby! You may feel you do not have their respect or their understanding of what it means to you. Rather than motivate and inspire you, they may even consider what you are doing an interruption to the normal running of the family home, and they may complain. This is why it is important, in the planning stages, to discuss your business plans with your partner—get them on your side right from the word go. At the very least, ask them to let you give it a fair go.

As a coach, and your own boss, you can work the hours that best suit you and your family. It may mean a couple of hours in the morning and afternoon, and in the evening you may have to spend a couple of hours in your office working on your business marketing plans or doing evening calls. You may also have to be prepared to work around and fit in with your family—who should be your priority in the first place! If you don't give your family reason to feel they are taking second place to your business, you won't experience the problems that others face when they make their families take second place to their businesses. We, Terri Levine, Larina Kase, and Joe

Vitale, are blessed with family support, which, we happily acknowledge, makes being a huge success so much easier!

You can even hire your own coach while you are becoming a coach yourself or trying to build up your practice. You will find it much easier to be successful if you have your own coach, and you will have all the support and encouragement you need and then some! For example, Larina is a business coach and knows how to grow a business. So why would she hire a business coach of her own? Because having a coach is invaluable in offering support, guidance, ideas, and inspiration for ongoing growth. And we keep telling you, if the experts are doing it, it must be worth doing!

## The Intimidating World of Marketing

One of the most common fears that holds coaches and consultants or wannabe coaches and consultants back is to do with marketing. Terri's coach-training program includes marketing, but we're aware that many programs do not. People don't know what to do. They don't want to spend and waste money and time on marketing that doesn't work. They can't afford to hire marketing gurus to do it for them. Any marketing that involves having to go out and meet people face-to-face makes some people shrivel up and look for the nearest rock to crawl under.

Fear of marketing will contribute to self-sabotaging behavior. This will show up if you don't believe you know how to market, you don't believe you can do it effectively, you believe marketing strategies must be very expensive and unaffordable, you believe only famous people can market their own products or services effectively, or you quite simply cringe at the idea of having to promote yourself and your service. If this is you, relax. You're in experienced hands, and we will help you overcome the fears and feel confident about your marketing abilities.

Now you have plenty of food for thought about the many things that are stopping you or could stop you from becoming a top coach. Start your list. We'll tackle them together.

### Interview with Patsi Krakoff, Psy.D.

Dr. Krakoff helps independent professionals, including coaches, leverage the Internet and create automated systems to help build business and get clients. This includes newsletters, blogs, and other systems. Visit her web sites http://www.CustomizedNewsletters.com and http://www.coachezines.com. She and business partner Denise Wakeman have a web site known as the Blog Squad at http://www.buildabetterblog.com.

**How did your coaching career develop?**
I knew as soon as I finished postgraduate internship work that I didn't want to work with ill or dysfunctional individuals. At the time, working with well people meant either organizational/industrial or sports psychology, neither of which I had studied.

I searched on the Internet, and I discovered the coaching industry in its infancy. I was attracted to the idea of working with "normal" people, helping them to take themselves to their next level. It wasn't until years later that Dr. Martin Seligman and other psychologists formed a branch of study called positive psychology. Ironically, he is now teaching that model of helping people through one of the leading coach training schools!

I worked as a coach for several years and did coach newsletters as a sideline, writing articles which I sold to other coaches who didn't want to use their time to write their own newsletters.

In 2003, my husband and I moved to Mexico to try out a softer way of living. I gave up everything I couldn't do on the 'Net, including coaching individuals, in favor of developing my Customized Newsletter Services. That turned out to be a surprising revelation to me, as I enjoyed putting my energies into reading, researching, writing, and helping others market themselves via the Internet, much more than actual coaching!

Today we are back in the United States, and my coaching consists of helping other professionals use newsletters, blogs, shopping carts, info products, and the Internet to grow business.

A nontechie by nature, I have since learned HTML coding, how to use e-commerce and shopping-cart systems, how to create

*(continued)*

and maintain blogging software, and how to create automated systems to run a professional practice with ease.

Let's face it, none of us were using e-mail 10 years ago. If I can learn to blog, change a web page, create an electronic e-zine, and update autoresponders and merchant purchases on the Internet, I figure anybody can!

It helps to find the right partner to fill in the gaps of your own talents, but the key here is to know what you're good at, what you love doing, and find others to do what you're not so good at, what you like least.

Denise Wakeman of http://www.nextlevelpartnership.com and http://www.biztipsblog.com has been the perfect match for me.

Professionals don't have to reinvent the wheel. They just have to get on the bus. Like the story says, you can't win the lottery if you don't buy a ticket. Don't get caught up in the frenzy of marketing and Internet gurus who want your money more than they want you to succeed.

For me, I had to spend some money and take some tele-courses, and I had to read many e-books to get up to speed on what was needed to be successful. It's not only about helping others to succeed. You must help yourself to succeed by having marketing systems in place.

**As a psychologist, you are an expert in identifying thoughts and behaviors. What is the mind game of highly successful coaches?**

Aha, good questions! Successful coaches, in my humble opinion, possess two important and essential qualities:

**1.** They are serenely self-confident.
**2.** They are deeply in love with people—both as individuals and as humanity.

If you are someone who is introverted, introspective, questioning, and shy, coaching is not for you. I don't care how smart, how polished, how educated, and how well you interact with people. You'll be playing with the deck stacked against you. Your work as a coach will be an effort instead of a positive flow.

I see too many good psychologists trying to become successful as a coach, but who lack these two essential qualities. Psychologists, and many therapists and "helping professionals," are often introspective and have studied the psyche, both their own and others', to the point of requiring a deep understanding of what makes the client tick. This is a waste of time for a successful coach. Understanding fully the inner world of the client is a need for the psychologist, not for the successful coach.

A successful coach really loves people and is deeply interested in each client. Self-confidence and love of others is not something that can be taught (although you can study it and emulate it, but if it is not authentic, it will be a lot of work).

**What holds coaches back from being successful?**
Either they don't have enough education, or they have too much!

In the first case, many individuals feel that because they have conquered some challenges in their own lives, they can automatically help others by becoming a coach. And they can, as long as each client is exactly like them, and that isn't going to happen!

In this case, what will hold them back is a lack of understanding about other human beings and what makes them tick.

In the second case—of too much education—I am addressing those coaches who have a well-rounded education, experience, and understanding of what makes people tick (therapists, nurses, psychologists, and others, for example) and who attempt to transition into a coaching practice. These people are highly educated and have valuable experience in working with individuals of all kinds.

But they lack knowledge of what it takes to run a business. They have never had to market themselves. They have little know-how in how to drive clients to find them on the web or on the phone or in teleseminars.

Having a successful coaching business means you have a steady stream of clients coming to you through an association with a business or a school or something, or you are in

*(continued)*

the newspapers and on the Internet or radio or "out there" so people can find you.

There has to be some thought put into marketing yourself: a brand, a name, a logo, and some information about you in the form of newsletters, blogs, e-books, free reports that are easily accessible to people who might want to hire you.

Many people who want to be successful at coaching haven't done the groundwork or put it off. Some of them love being around people so much that they put their energies into networking but leave no paper trail, have no way to collect e-mail addresses, and aren't building a database to market to.

**Why is niche marketing so important for coaches?**
Do you think a bar of soap would sell if it were marked *bar of soap*? Why would you hire someone who is *a coach*? When you go into the music store, you can find what you want right away by category. In a world where there are so many products and people, you must differentiate yourself. Nobody is going to hire you without knowing, or at least feeling, that you are the one coach who can help.

This is a problem for well-educated people because they can do so much and don't want to cut themselves off from others by narrowing their niche.

First of all, you can't create a brand, a logo, a company name, an e-zine name, or a web site identity if you are *all things to all people.* You can, but just how catchy, how memorable is it to call yourself *a coach*?

Ah, yes, but what if you were the Blog Squad? That's what I'm talking about, something catchy and memorable. Yes, I know, Customized Newsletters is a little bland and boring for a web site and company name, but I wanted something that says what it is. The point is you need to create a name, a logo, colors, and informational products just as if you were a bar of soap. You can't do that until you sit down and think about what exactly is it that you do for your clients, what benefits they derive from working with you. Until you are clear and specific about what you do and how you do it, you can't create a name or brand with all the marketing pizzazz that goes with it. You may have lots of meat but no sizzle.

The problem many coaches have today is a lack of brand identity. They are too generic and too all-encompassing.

**What are some tips for helping coaches create and market a niche for themselves?**
Coaches, know thyself. Niche thyself. Brand thyself. Market the heck out of thyself.

If you need help, get it. Follow your own advice. There are so many people who specialize in helping other coaches get to where they want and need to go that there is only one excuse if you fail. If you fail to create and market a niche for yourself, it is because of only one thing: *You don't want it bad enough!*

If money is an issue, try partnering up with someone and coach each other.

If time is an issue, try a half hour a day of targeted work on your goals, then review your progress each week. Using a coach/buddy often helps stay on track. If you make excuses to yourself, you know how easy that is to "revise" your goals. It's harder to do when you are accountable to a coach/buddy.

If self-confidence is an issue, you may be trying to do a profession that is not ideal for you. If you don't sincerely love working with people, you maybe shouldn't try to be a coach.

Most professionals transitioning into coaching have spent a great deal of money, time, and energy learning how to coach through one of the training schools. That is a good start. Your coach training will only take you so far.

To be a successful coach means you are in two businesses:

1. Coaching.
2. Marketing.

*(continued)*

Spend time and money learning how to market yourself, including branding issues, including niche specialization. Then learn how to automate your marketing systems.

No coach can afford to spend her/his time sending out e-mails to stay in touch with people. There must be a system in place with autoresponders, downloadable informational products, and newsletters. There must be a place where people can go to on the web to learn more about you and your services. This can be a web site or even a blog. A blog can do most everything a web site can do, and it costs less and is user-friendly (no web designer necessary).

There must be a way for potential clients to leave their e-mail address with you in exchange for an assessment or some other information so that you can build a list of people who would like to hear from you on a regular basis.

Don't know how to do this? Don't worry. None of us knew how to do all these things 5 or 10 years ago! You don't have to be a techie. These days, there are systems available that even nontechies like me can run and maintain.

If you want to know more about these things, drop me an e-mail at patsi@customizednewsletters.com or visit one of my blogs and participate by leaving a comment. If you have needs in the areas of newsletters, blogs, shopping carts, or more, either Denise or I can help you, and it won't cost an arm or a leg. We have a number of free reports and minicourses to get you started.

# 3

# Conquer Excuses That Stand in Your Path

*The first and the best victory is to conquer self.*

— Plato

*"I don't have a fancy education. What do I know about starting a business?"*

*"I'm so busy! I just don't have the time to learn something new!"*

*"There are so many coaches out there already and they're much smarter than I am!"*

*"I don't know if I'm clever enough to learn how to do it."*

*"I can't afford the lessons."*

*"I can't afford to start a business. Doesn't it cost a lot of money?"*

*"What if I'm no good? I can't afford to lose all that money and it will be hard to get my old job back."*

*"People will see right through me. I can't coach CEOs!"*

*"I probably wouldn't get any clients and my family will say 'I told you so!'"*

*"I'm not technology savvy. My lack of technology knowledge will limit my business growth!"*

No, we haven't been eavesdropping . . . we've heard it all before. Maybe you recognize some of these excuses. Maybe you use them. If you've been toying with the idea of coaching or consulting work and you do nothing about it, then something is holding you back, and it can be one or more of these fears.

And you know what else? You're being your own worst enemy. You are doubting yourself and selling yourself short. We all make excuses for not pursuing things with 100 percent gusto and commitment.

Realize that any form of self-sabotage is all in the mind. You lack confidence in yourself and your abilities. You make excuses so you don't have to put yourself to the test, because *you* believe you will fail! Or maybe you're just not quite convinced that you won't fail.

Would it surprise you to learn that you are in good company? Self-sabotage is really quite common. Everybody is affected by it in some way or another, for one reason or another. They'd love to learn to dance but they don't have the time or the money, they're afraid they'll be no good and make a fool of themselves in public, and so on. So they don't even try in the first place. What a shame if it turned out they were really rather good at it! Not that they will find out because they don't give themselves the chance!

We're not saying self-sabotage is behind every reason you have not achieved something you have dreamed about, but it is a very common phenomenon.

Maybe there are other reasons you have put off trying because you just can't seem to get yourself going. You make excuses—some of which may be very real excuses! Maybe you really don't have spare funds, but have you endeavored to explore payment-plan possibilities? Special loans? A savings plan? A barter system?

## Who's Making the Excuses?

The truth about excuses is that you really can't blame outside influences or circumstances or people. You are the one holding yourself back. Nobody else! It's a personal decision. And who are you to decide that what you know is not valuable to others?

There are as many coaching niches as there are coaches. You don't have to have a university education. Are you good with teenagers? Are you good with relationships? Are you good at organizing time and household matters? Are you a career woman with a family who has learned how to balance everything so you can succeed at both on your own terms? Realize there are thousands of people out there who would love your expertise and experience! As a life coach, you can help them.

The techniques of excuse making can creep up on you in subtle, sneaky ways, until one day you are not even aware you are doing it. It's become second nature. A way of life. Maybe in other aspects of life you are doing very well, so the odd excuse for not doing something doesn't stand out.

You might say to yourself, "It doesn't matter about that because I already have a good job. I have a great life. I don't need anything else." Don't you? Would you if you could? Are you kidding yourself? You know, all of us can do better if we really want to. Are you settling for second best because it is easier? Why have a mediocre life when you can have a fantastic life?

Can you imagine, for just a second, that your excuses are like a pair of blackened sunglasses, obscuring your view. Imagine taking those glasses off and seeing the myriad opportunities lying in front of you. Imagine if you could pick any opportunity you wanted. Wouldn't you want to if it meant immense happiness and a double serving of everything wonderful you imagine life to be? By keeping those blackened sunglasses on, do you see how you are not allowing yourself to grow and experience all that life has to offer?

You don't have to go down the most difficult path. You will find other paths, not so difficult, that will still reach the destination where some of your life's dreams lie. You can take baby steps toward them. With your dark glasses on, you don't move anywhere. Sure, that is safe, but when you're 80 years old and look back on your life, will you regret not having tried? Will you regret the wasted moments in life? Might you say, "I wish I had given that a go, but now it's too late."

## Identifying Patterns That Are Fueled by Excuses

Do you recognize any of these behaviors or habits?

- You hate your job, yet you stay there, year after year, miserable and wishing things were different.
- You keep doing the same things time after time, even if they don't work, because they are familiar. You keep repeating the same mistakes.
- You'd like to improve your relationship with your child, spouse, or parent, but something—pride, stubbornness—holds you

back, and you can't bring yourself to express how you truly feel.

- You avoid situations in which you might land in the limelight or be expected to speak publicly.
- You hate where you live but cannot bring yourself to move.
- Any form of change unsettles you, even if there is no valid reason for the feeling.
- You'd love to try scuba diving, but you've seen *Jaws* too many times!

We could keep adding to this list, but we think you get the picture. Do you see how these behaviors hold people back from experiencing better relationships, more fun in their lives, more joy?

Please don't feel defensive. You'd be surprised to learn that the majority of the population engages in these types of excuse-driven behaviors in one way or another. As far as human nature goes, it's normal. Not ideal, but quite normal.

You'd be surprised to learn the number of entrepreneurs who were once well-trained self-saboteurs, and some of them are still battling it even in the midst of increasing success and awareness.

Of course, any form of business venture has its risks, but you don't go mountain climbing with your eyes closed. You prepare. You do your homework and research. You give yourself every chance. You don't just jump into something spontaneously without preparation and a map or plan to guide you onward. You make sure you have savings behind you for the initial lean times. You make sure you have learned all you need to run your business and market it, otherwise you hire somebody who can take care of those aspects for you. Careful preparation can make the difference between success and failure, and knowing this, what is there to be afraid of? Are you afraid of success? (Don't laugh! Some people really are afraid of success, but that's another topic for another time!)

What you need to realize is that there is nothing certain in this life. You can't be certain you won't be hit by a bus next week or that your company won't downsize and you'll be out of a job anyway. You can't be certain of anything. One thing you can be certain of is if you don't do something different from what you always do, you'll stay in the same place getting the same stale results that you always do. A stale life. Is that appetizing?

Is it a fear of the unknown that is holding you back? Would you be pleasantly surprised to know that you can start your coaching business with nothing more than a telephone? Of course, having a computer and Internet connection will make life easier for you, but you don't *have* to have a computer straight away if you can't afford one. Most coaching takes place via telephone with clients—and they ring you, so you aren't going to be in for very large phone bills, either.

Having said that, part of your business plan should include a computer; it is easier to connect via e-mail. Although having a web site is not imperative, you may wish to use that as another medium for marketing your services, selling products, and communicating with your potential clients. You can work with virtual assistants who can do your bookwork, make your appointments, and perform myriad other tasks that you don't want to have to make time for or don't enjoy doing. But really, to start off, you just need a telephone. You can advertise in the printed media, and you can maintain your books the old-fashioned, manual way. We mention this to prove to you how little capital you need to start a coaching business. So poof, there goes the "I don't have enough money" excuse, right out the window!

## What If You Gave Up All the Excuses?

Don't buy into the well-meaning negativity of your friends and family. Don't listen to their fears. If you want to do something, do your own research and make up your own mind. Sometimes, the reality is much less frightening than what you were imagining. So many people assume that for all businesses you need a lot of expensive technological equipment and a mountain of money behind you before you can even open the doors, when, really, nothing could be farther from the truth. Want proof?

In 1976, two young men in their early twenties, Steve Jobs and Steve Wozniak, started Apple Computers in a garage. Six months later, they were sharing a monthly salary of just $250. Just one year later, they'd taken on a partner, Mike Markkula, who invested in their computer enterprise. The rest, as they say, is history.

Colonel Sanders started Kentucky Fried Chicken with his social security check! (Yes, having investors helped, too. These days, if you want investors, you'd better have your business plan prepared.)

And let's not forget Walt Disney! If he had let his bankruptcy stop him from chasing his dreams we wouldn't have Disneyland or any of the wonderful Disney animations and films that came out of the Disney stable.

And surely you've heard of Sir Richard Branson, founder and CEO of the Virgin empire. He was not an impressive student at school. He was dyslexic, but at the age of 17, he started a student newspaper. He dropped out of school to focus on that and one thing led to another.

Isn't it reassuring to know that people with unimpressive backgrounds can do incredible things, just by following their dreams?

Isn't it reassuring to know that despite seemingly huge stumbling blocks, people *can* succeed at whatever they put their mind to?

See what can happen if you don't let excuses hold you back?

## Technophobia: A Common Excuse

Are you familiar with voice mail? Are you familiar with computers and the software used? Do you know how to use a photocopier or send an e-fax? Can you create a PDF file? Can you create or at least manage the shopping cart on your web site? Do you know all the latest ways to use the Internet? Does just talking about this send shivers up your spine?

Ever say, "But I don't know how to use all the latest technology"? For many of us, technology takes us out of our comfort zone. It is constantly changing, and it is easy to feel like you are always behind. Many coaches we have coached had elaborate excuses and explanations about why technology held them back from coaching success.

As we said earlier, you don't have to spend a lot of money to set up a successful coaching practice, but sooner rather than later you will need a computer. There are things you can do with a computer that you just can't do by hand or on an old-fashioned typewriter. There are many affordable classes that teach the basics of using a computer and how to use the software. Maybe a neighbor or family member is computer literate and can spend a few hours with you, showing you the ropes? If you can't afford proper lessons, don't discount any teenagers you may know who probably do know how to use a computer and the software and would gladly show you for pocket money.

When you buy equipment, have the sales person show you how to use it before you get home. Some how-to manuals are not that easy to understand, and if you find you must do it yourself when you get home, think of friends or neighbors who might be able to help you and show you.

Don't let something that is so readily fixable (like not being technically minded) hold you back. If millions of people of all ages, races, backgrounds, and levels of education all around the world can use computers and fax machines and voice mail, then it stands to reason you can and will too. Just because you may be unfamiliar with something doesn't mean you cannot learn how to use it. The average video player is harder to figure out than the average piece of office equipment!

*Bear in mind that it doesn't matter how much equipment or resources you have access to. If you were asked, you'd probably still think you didn't have enough or you could think of many other things you would like to have. That's just the way it is. People always feel they never have enough money or enough time. Really, that is no excuse. It's not a matter of how much money or how much time you have, because if you really wanted to do or buy something, your brain could most certainly come up with a plan to achieve it.*

If you ever doubt this, just remember all those famous entrepreneurs who overcame great obstacles to get to where they are today. You are capable of this, too.

Let's explore another method of achieving the mental game of successful coaches: the right thoughts to replace the excuses. Want the mind of a millionaire coach? Read on.

# 4

# Thinking Like a Top Coach

*The thing that you believe is the very thing that you will become.*
—Larina Kase

Now you know how your excuses may be holding you back from becoming a top coach. So what's the solution? Learn how to overcome these types of thoughts and train your mind to think like the successful coach you have inside you! Sounds like a lot to do, but we're here to help. We'll walk you through the process of shaping your mind for success. Let's get started.

## Step One: Spot the Culprit!

Before you can defeat the enemy (whatever is holding you back), you must identify it. We need to find out what, specifically, is occurring for you. Is it an attitude, a belief, a behavior pattern? This may sound simple, but beware! Some negative thoughts and self-talk occur so automatically that you are not even aware of their presence. You've been doing it for so long that it has become second nature to you.

Do friends ever make the comment, "Stop putting yourself down"? And you weren't even aware that you were? They have just identified one of your self-sabotage techniques for you. The rest you will have to hunt down yourself.

### It's More Than Positive Thinking

How we think influences who we are and who we become. It affects our moods, reactions, and behaviors. Negative, self-put-down thoughts make us feel miserable and gloomy. Positive, proud thoughts of ourselves make us soar!

You can see, then, that when you sit down to study your coaching program, if you are feeling grumpy, just had an argument, feeling bad about yourself, whatever, you won't be feeling inspired or motivated to study.

Don't be fooled by thinking that positive thoughts are good and negative thoughts are bad. It is not as simple as just think more positively. What we want to help you do is think more *accurately*. Creating your own coaching business is an intimidating thing, ripe with anxiety. When we are nervous, our thoughts become clouded by fear. We can become overwhelmed by self-doubt, negative predictions, and reduced confidence. We will help you uncloud your thinking and create the most accurate, helpful thoughts possible.

### How to Spot the Unhelpful Thoughts

Often it is easier to notice what mood you are in rather than the specific thoughts flashing through your mind. Until you learn to control your thoughts, you can use your mood as an indicator and adjust your thinking accordingly.

Noticing your negative thoughts will take practice. Sometimes they come so quickly your conscious mind doesn't even realize the thought has occurred! You can practice "thought catching" by writing down your thoughts each time you notice them. You have to be on your toes and have the intent of noticing them when you have them.

Writing down these thoughts has the same effect as when you wake up and quickly record your dreams. You do it straight away, otherwise they are soon forgotten and this information is lost to you. This is important because it will help you become more aware of them, to know exactly what they are, and to work to change them. We will get into that later.

Here's a tool to help you. Larina Kase recommends that her coaching clients record their thoughts for two weeks to become aware of the patterns that occur and has outlined in the following section how it works and how to use it. Be particularly aware of your thoughts as you are working on your coaching business. As you begin to think about your project (whether it be writing a marketing plan, studying, or authoring your first e-book), record the situations and all of your thoughts in the first and second columns.

| Situation | Negative Thought | Label |
|---|---|---|
| | | |
| | | |
| | | |
| | | |
| | | |

## Step Two: Identify the Culprit!

As you're reading through this section, think how you can begin identifying how these thought patterns come up for you. You can also consider how you can help your clients learn these ideas. This works. Using this tool, Larina has helped some of her executive and business-coaching clients recognize and overcome these types of thoughts that stood in the way of their career success. Once they changed their thinking patterns, there was nothing holding them back from meeting their career and business goals. If you have clients who become nervous about their work and whose thinking sabotages their success, the book written by Larina Kase, with a foreword by Joe Vitale, *Anxious Nine to Five: How to Beat Worry, Stop Second Guessing Yourself, and Work with Confidence* (New Harbinger, 2006), could help them.

After you have written down your thoughts, the next step is to *label the thought*. Aaron Beck, a master cognitive therapist, identified many types of thoughts that lead to negative emotions such as anxiety or depression. Specific types of thinking (which may not be entirely rational) often lead to self-sabotaging fears and beliefs. Beck and his colleagues (1976) describe a number of cognitive distortions, which include the following:

### Magnification

This is seeing a situation (or aspects of it) as much more horrible than it really is.

*This is when you begin to think that you have absolutely no credibility or expertise to be a coach. Another example is how you magnify one weaker part of your understanding in your training and decide that the whole exercise is a failure because you don't like that one section.*

### Minimization

Glossing over or underestimating your ability to cope well with a difficult situation.

*This is when you think that if your marketing is not successful right away, you will not be able to deal with it, instead of thinking about how well you have dealt with other challenging situations and what you could do to improve your marketing. Minimization may also make you forget how you can have other people (colleagues, consultants, coaches) help you if you do not know everything yourself.*

### All or None Thinking

Believing that you are either a totally competent Superman or Wonder Woman or that you are a completely incompetent mess. Looking at things as black and white and ignoring all the shades of gray in between.

*This cognitive error is very common with self-sabotage. This is when you tell yourself that if it is not going to be an incredible success, it isn't even worth trying. Or that you either are a coach or you are not a coach. You may think that you either need to be a fantastic marketer or that you should not even bother.*

### Personalization

Overidentifying with (imagining yourself in) situations or potential problems without good reason.

*This is assuming that although other people can be successful at coaching, it is unlikely that you will be successful. It sets up a me-versus-them type of thinking in which you assume that others can be excellent coaches or marketers but that you will not. This is in contrast to the mindset of abundance. You can create a competitive mindset that is unlikely to help you succeed as a coach.*

### Selective Attention

Focusing mostly or entirely on threatening or frightening aspects of a situation while ignoring the relevant context around the situation. Remembering only the situations that have been difficult to cope with and forgetting those times in which you coped well. This is like tunnel vision. You hone in on one or two problems and become so distracted by them that you forget all of the good things that you have going.

*You are so worried about the technical aspects of creating or marketing that you lose sight of the fact that you have a great idea and that you are a great coach. You become so preoccupied with thinking that no one will hire you and that you will fail that you overlook all the times in which you have been successful.*

### Fortune-Telling

Assuming you know the future and that it will be negative in a major way, even if your fear has not happened or is unlikely to happen.

*This is another big one for new coaches and consultants. You predict the future as if you have a crystal ball. You say to yourself, "No one is going to hire me," or "People will think that I am a fraud trying to sell myself as an expert." In reality, you do not know these things, but your fear is making these predictions feel very real.*

This type of thinking can be particularly problematic because it can become a self-fulfilling prophecy. When we predict a specific outcome, that outcome is often what we make happen. A great quote to illustrate this idea is:

Whether you think you can or think you can't, you're right.

—*Henry Ford*

### Overgeneralization

Seeing an upsetting incident as proof of a negative pattern that you assume will stretch indefinitely into the future.

*You may have tried coaching or consulting in the past, and it did not take off and become the instant success you had hoped. You then assume that any business that you try to build in the future will be similarly unsuccessful. You take one incident or situation and overgeneralize it and apply it to future situations that may bear no resemblance to that one incident.*

### Emotional Reasoning

Assuming that it is true because you *feel* like it is. Reasoning based on your emotions rather than an objective reality.

*An example of emotional reasoning is thinking that because you feel worried about how your business will do, it is unlikely to do well. Our thoughts become irrational when they are clouded by emotions. Another common example of emotional reasoning is thinking that a workshop or speech that you gave went horribly because you felt anxious.*

*Probability Overestimation*

Exaggerating your predictions of the likelihood of a horrible future event or assuming that everyone will respond a certain way when in reality only a few or none of the people will respond negatively.

*This is saying to yourself, "Everyone will think I'm a fraud and that I have nothing new to offer." In reality, some people may think that because they are coaching junkies who have studied it themselves or had a series of their own coaches and will make comparisons (not likely to happen unless you venture into a niche in which you are inexperienced or untrained), but most people probably would not have any coach training or even hired a coach before and have none of these types of thoughts.*

*You may predict that it is 99 percent likely that your coaching or consulting business will be a flop. The reality may not be 0 percent, but it is unlikely to be 99 percent. If it were 25 percent likely that your business would not be as huge as you would have liked, would it be worth the risk of doing something that you really believed in? Probably.*

Now go back up to the thoughts that you wrote down previously and label the type of cognitive distortion or self-sabotaging thinking that may be coming into play. As an example:

| Situation | Negative Thought | Label |
| --- | --- | --- |
| Brainstorming niche ideas | "No one will hire me for this" | Fortune-telling |
| Thinking about studying | "I have not followed through with projects in the past, why will this be different?" | Overgeneralization |
| About to sit down at the computer | "Who am I to try to do this?" | Personalization |

## Time to Change Your Thinking!

It takes 21 days to make a habit and 21 days to break a habit—give or take a day! You'll notice many self-hypnosis and self-help tapes want you to listen for at least 21 days, and this is the reason why. The power to transform your life and your mind is within you, and with the right tools, it can be as easy as falling off a log. Here's one tool that helps many people now: Comprehensive Coaching U Brain-Speak Program at http://www.terrilevine.com/brainspeak.htm. (You will find other excellent tools used by Terri Levine, Larina Kase, and Joe Vitale in the Recommended Resources at the back of this book.)

In addition to changing habits, you can also change the way you think. Studies have proved that when you learn to overcome your negative thinking and replace these thoughts with positive thoughts, the negative thoughts will show up less and less. You will feel better and your self-confidence will improve.

If you keep a record of your negative thoughts over the course of a few days or even weeks, you will see a pattern emerge. You will be able to look at your list and identify:

- Your most common fears or thoughts.
- Does any one particular thought occur more than the others?
- When do these negative thoughts occur most often?
- Are there any specific situations that trigger these thoughts for you?

Once you know the situations that are likely to trigger these types of thoughts, you can be on the lookout for them. When you recognize them, you can then do something about them.

There is more than one technique available for instilling positive thoughts, and one of them is saying affirmations. This involves repeating sentences on a daily basis that instill positive thoughts and images into your brain. These can be anything from, "Every day in every way I am getting better and better." Or "I am confident and capable of learning and doing new things, and I do so easily." They are positive thought suggestions you give yourself every day until they take root in your mind. Give yourself a pep talk. Talk to yourself about the things in which you excel or are clever. Build yourself up. Lift your spirits. Find all the great things you can about yourself and pat yourself on the back. Get your mood *up*.

People use affirmations to help them change their lives by first changing their thinking. They use them like a mantra, repeating the positive suggestions over and over to themselves. You can't rely on affirmations alone to create the permanent changes you seek, however. They are one tool to use but are often not enough on their own.

The problem for many people is that their beliefs are so deeply ingrained that simply repeating to themselves the opposite belief is not enough to make it stick. This is because the opposite, positive statement is such a radical change for you that it's too unbelievable. Saying an affirmation and noticing your resistant response can help you uncover your real fears. You can then recognize whether any of the previously mentioned thought patterns are at work.

You may find you have to start with affirmation statements that are slightly more believable for you and work your way up. For example, if your negative belief is that you will always be poor and never make enough money, it probably will be too much for your mind to accept or find credible a positive statement that says, "I am a multimillionaire and own a string of yachts." You might have to start with "I have plenty of money for all my needs and wants" and build up from there.

As with any activity, you need to train. In this case, you need to train your thoughts to respond differently in situations in which you are usually negative. It will take practice and persistence, but it can be done with the process that you will learn in this book.

## You Be the Jury

As mentioned, with some very strong thoughts, just relying on positive-thinking replacement may not be effective because your brain doubts its credibility and cannot accept the new, stronger, positive statement. All is not lost, however. There is another, very effective way to change your beliefs.

A great way to do this is to challenge your thoughts. Pretend you are presenting two sides of an argument—for and against the thought—to a jury. One side of the argument is for your negative thought, and the other side is an argument against your original thought. This helps you to begin looking at the situation more objectively.

Start by asking yourself, "What is the evidence that supports this thought or indicates it is true?" If the thought is "No one will be interested in what I have to say," then come up with evidence from your experience that this idea is true:

1. *When I told a few friends about my business niche idea, they did not have anything to say, they didn't seem very interested. One even rolled his eyes!*
2. *I wrote a couple of articles on a similar topic and had difficulty finding an interested editor.*
3. *When I gave a lecture on this topic, a few people in the audience gave me feedback that the topic was not very interesting.*

*4. My parents used to tell me that I never have anything important to con-tribute. So clearly, this is just another example of that!*

*5. A colleague told me to consider adding some more research to my studies to make my skills stronger. Implying I'm weak? Not ready?*

Now, write down an alternative thought to your original thought: "Many people will be very interested in what I have to offer." Then, ask yourself, "What is all of the evidence that this alternative thought is true?" You might say:

*1. I conducted an online survey and also asked my own mailing list for their opinions, and approximately 85 percent said that they would be interested in this service.*

*2. Many things that I have done in the past have gone over very well and received excellent reviews.*

*3. Several past clients have asked me to present this topic to their group.*

*4. I have been successful in several endeavors in the past, even when I was afraid that they would fail.*

*5. I can remember at least five times when I thought people would not be interested in something that I wrote or said, only to have great feedback and encouragement.*

Pretend you are the judge, the jury, the prosecuting attorney, and the defense attorney. It is your task to present both sides honestly and objectively and then evaluate the evidence for both sides and reach a verdict.

After looking at the evidence for both sides, decide the likelihood of the original fear actually being true.

The original thought has about a 25 percent likelihood of being true. So you say, "Before this process, I *felt 100 percent sure* that no one will be interested in what I have to say, and afterward I felt 25 percent sure. Is it worth the risk if I am only 25 percent sure? Yes!"

You can then produce an alternative idea. For instance, "Some people will not be interested, but many probably will be interested" or "Enough people will be interested to make this worth doing."

One of the reasons that this process for changing your thoughts and beliefs is so effective is that it helps you look at your ideas in a more objective way. Thoughts that are driven by fear are going to show the cognitive distortions described previously.

Another game you can play is to pretend your best friend has come to you with that thought. Are you going to agree and tell them what a loser they are, or are you going to help them rationalize their thinking and point out the positive? We look at our friends' situations more objectively; we are much harder on ourselves.

Learning how to take a step back and evaluate our thoughts with the strong negative emotion taken out of the picture can show us that the initial reactions are not always the most accurate *and* that it is often a good idea not to act on a strong negative emotion. This will open you up to getting started with your coaching business as effectively as possible, which brings us to the next point.

### Interview with Angus McLeod

Angus is a very inspirational person and coach and active on the world stage. He is the author of numerous papers on coaching in the international press and books including *Performance Coaching: The Handbook for Managers, HR Professionals and Coaches* (Bancyfelin, Carmarthen, UK: Crown House, 2003) and *Me, Myself, My Team: How to Become an Effective Team Player Using NLP* (Bancyfelin, Carmarthen, UK: Crown House, 2001). His organization's web site is http://www.angusmcleod.com.

**Why are coaches' belief systems important in their coaching careers?**
Beliefs, like emotions, are motivators and demotivators of action. Both are key to moving forward—indeed, a coach would be a poor role model if they had inadequate personal understanding of motivation, commitment, and action. A career is predicated by action, and hence beliefs that are sensible, holistic, aligned, and allow the prospect of "stretch" have to be vital to make a positive change in career, just as elsewhere.

**What are some of the limiting beliefs you have seen that have held coaches back?**
Coaches sometimes feel that they have to know an enormous amount about coaching tools in order to coach, and this can hold some good coaches back. It is critical to have a set of key

skills and that these are properly perfected in training and practice sessions with colleagues. But the core impact of coaches is less about capabilities and more about authentic core values and beliefs. If these are truly authentic, then they manifest as actions in the world. It is worth mentioning those "coaches" who are overly confident as well!

Some of these are so involved with their own "brilliance" and so enthusiastic about their newly honed skills that they attend less well to the coachee than is useful. It does not matter that the coach is good or not, it matters that the coachee is inspired to learning and action in the presence of their coach. A good coach will take quiet satisfaction from that after the session.

### How are the things that coaches fear often the very things that can make the coaching highly effective (for example, silence)?

Many coaches, at all levels, are fearful of silence or feel "responsible for keeping a conversation going" during their so-called coaching. But it is always in the silence that the most momentous perceptions and commitments take place. These cathartic moments can be lost if the coach does not learn to be comfortable with silence and use it to the coachee's advantage.

Almost no one teaches or demonstrates the importance of silence in coaching. I have been facilitating what we call "The Power of Silence" in many locations and rarely meet coaches who have previous understanding of the enormous power of silence in coaching, in spite of weeks of training. It is a terrible omission and serves their customers badly.

### How can authenticity help a coach overcome some of her or his fears?

I do not know of any quick route to self-development and theacquiring of authenticity and grace. Sure, there are areas in which a person can concentrate and get help with their development, but simply taking on a set of beliefs is not enough. To re-pose your question, authenticity does not diminish fears, it is the letting go of fears that is part of the journey to authenticity.

*(continued)*

In the world we get very hooked up on what we "do," and hence our sense of identity can get very skewed toward action. But we also have to learn to give credit to positive traits of "being" (without necessary outcomes).

How does that work? One question I often ask is, "When you succeeded in that, what was it about the personality of you that made a difference to the way that you succeeded?" In other words, people succeed in different ways—some will scratch and stride over others to achieve and others will harness motivations and succeed by gaining the support of a team. By attending to the positive qualities of self in all actions, coaches begin to honor the quality of their "being" to a greater extent. This leads to increased self-confidence and to improved authenticity. And that means credibility, believability, impact, and success.

**What advice do you have for coaches who are just starting out or who are dedicated to building their coaching businesses?**
Be expert in a set of coaching tools. You do not need that many, but be expert with them. Attend fully to the coachee and trust that if you need an intervention that it will come; keep your head clear to give exquisite attention to your coachee at all times. Let clients and coachees understand what your style of coaching involves practically and be overt about the use of silence in coaching as a natural part of what you do—and remember that the coachee will think their two minutes of silence was less than 15 seconds!

Think about the networks and tertiary skills that you have and seek a sector in which you can make a mark by concentrating your effort in that sector. People will talk to one another about a big fish in a small pond, and your business will grow through less marketing effort. If you have not had training in counseling, Gestalt, psychotherapy, and so forth, then consider it. This will raise your game and improve your status. Force yourself to develop by placing yourself in the stretch zone. Do what you should be instilling in your coaches—decide to act, achieve, and then take time to honor your achievements and the qualities of you that impacted on your journey to success.

# 5

# Getting Started and Successful Studying Strategies

*Defeat is not the worst of failures. Not to have tried is the true failure.*
— George E. Woodberry

It sounds simple. You decide "I'd like to be a coach." Working from home, my own hours, and earning a nice income sounds terrific. You could go to the Internet and look up schools and make inquiries, decide on a payment plan for the training, start marketing your business for clients, and you're on your way.

Yet you don't. Week after week, the thought occurs to you, "That would be a nifty business to be in. I love helping people, and how great would it be to do that from home and actually get paid for it!" But you do nothing. You just can't get started. Why? You have fears holding you back. You aren't focused on your goals and dreams. You lack motivation, and you'll do anything to put off having to actually commit yourself.

## The First Steps Are the Hardest

Taking that first step is one of the biggest hurdles to overcome to commence the journey toward achieving your goals. For some, even if they make a start and get the information they need, something holds them back, and they lose momentum. The information sits on their desks gathering dust.

## Fear Holds You Back

Even though you may have more reasons for wanting to get started than you do for not wanting to get started, you still can't seem to do it. You continue to put it off and avoid taking that next step.

Again, you may be holding yourself back with negative self-talk and unfounded fears. Maybe you think, "What's the point of becoming a coach? What niche would I choose? I don't know anything special? Who would hire me?" Maybe you fear you'll lack credibility due to your level of experience or education. Maybe you fear you don't have enough time or money to learn and get started. Maybe you are kidding yourself and saying, "Sure, I'll do it . . . when I have more time (or money)."

With new coaches, a common fear is "What do I have to offer? Who is going to pay me to coach them?"

Where is your self-confidence? In your shoes? So what if you don't have a university degree! You can coach people in niches that don't require a high-level education. There are coaches who coach in niches like time management, organizational skills, work-life balance, and so on. In fact, if you feel that way—and we know hundreds of people do—there's a coaching niche for you right there. If you can overcome your lack of confidence and break through your self-sabotage barriers, you have the perfect experience and background to coach others to do the same!

Fear is only appropriate when you are faced with a real threat. If you are swimming and there is a shark in the water, your fear will motivate you to get out of the water fast—and save your life. Sometimes, fear freezes us, too, and we're unable to move. Think of an animal—a deer or rabbit—frozen in fear as your car approaches and you catch it in your headlights. But fear of starting a business or learning new skills doesn't make sense. It may *feel* dangerous, but is it really? Your life isn't at risk. You can't be harmed. In fact, you stand to gain from the experience.

Of course, you aren't likely to experience the adrenaline rush of a fight-or-flight response when considering starting a coaching career, but the freezing element may hit you. This is why it's so hard to get rolling.

Don't be afraid that you lack the expertise needed for coaching work. Don't let the fear that others will laugh at you if you say, for example, "I coach people to stop biting their fingernails" hold you back. (We personally have never heard of a coach in that niche, but you never know, maybe there *is* a need for that!) If you believe you have nothing to offer, then of course you won't get started. You'll think, "Why bother!"

There are secretaries and administrative workers who become coaches and coach others at their level to start their own virtual assistant work-from-home businesses. Career coaching is one of the most enjoyable niches in the industry, and you don't need a university degree to do that. In fact, for many coaching niches, you don't need a university degree; you just need to learn how to coach!

Personal trainers are getting coaching certification so they can offer more to their clients. They don't want to teach their clients only how to do push-ups, they want to motivate them to improve all areas of their clients' lives and motivate them to return each week to keep doing push-ups for their health. Ditto for yoga instructors. Terri Levine knows a work-from-home Herbalife distributor (who was a hairdresser in her past life) who is getting coaching training so she can motivate her clients to continue their health plans.

Coaches are not therapists or counselors. You don't work with clients on serious mental-health issues like depression and panic disorder. You don't need a doctorate to coach in the way that a psychologist needs a doctorate degree. The client's life is not in your hands—it is in their hands. If you have a coaching client who begins discussing issues that are more appropriate for therapy, you give a referral. It is neither necessary nor ethical to go beyond your competency area.

Coaches are not consultants. You don't have to tell anybody to do anything. You aren't the one who must come up with any solutions. You merely coach your clients to find the best solution for their situation and assist them in finding ways to help them achieve that goal. You will learn how when you get coach training, which we'll talk about some more soon.

Don't waste too much time and effort wondering what niche you'd coach in—the possibilities are limitless—and if you spend too much time worrying about this aspect, you'll never get started! Why not start the process then allow yourself to view all your possibilities once your training starts? You may be amazed to discover in just how many niches you *are* qualified to coach! Don't assume anything. Get your facts first!

# Delaying Getting Started

If this isn't holding you back, maybe you are simply procrastinating. Maybe you have bought a coaching kit that enables you to study at home, but each time you sit down to study, something happens to distract you. This needn't be an outside distraction. It may come from you! You open your coaching manual and then start thinking about cleaning the attic! Maybe you think, "Gee, if I have time to sit here reading this, I have time to polish the silver!"

Keep in mind the reason you are studying. It's for your future. It's for your new career. Polishing the silver *can* wait; that really is something you can do anytime. Why not think instead, "Gee, if I have time to polish the silver, I certainly have time to sit down and study a chapter in my coaching manual!" After all, the silver isn't going to make you any money, unless you sell it!

Maybe you sit down at your computer and start browsing coach-training schools to get information and find yourself getting sidetracked by other web sites you come across. Then, hours later, you look at the clock and think, "Wow! All this time has passed and I still haven't got the information I set out to get! Where did the time go!"

You need to remain focused on what it is you are doing. If there is another web site that fascinates you and you really want to explore it, write down or save the web address so you can go back and look at it later. Don't let it interfere with the reason you are there in the first place: to get information on coach training. First things first!

If lack of motivation is holding you back, and your partner, if you have one, is not exactly 100 percent supportive or thinks you are wasting your time, then this will hold you back, too. Having someone believe in you and encourage you can be very helpful. (And there's another coaching skill with which you can help others!) Some people really have difficulty motivating themselves.

Maybe you put off making a phone call or sending an e-mail to inquire about coaching programs because you figure you'll just watch a bit of TV first and then you'll make the call or send the e-mail. Of course, watching TV is just another excuse you are using to avoid getting started. Haven't you ever noticed that when you have a big job to do as well as several smaller ones, you tend to do the smaller ones first and put off doing the large job until you've finished the others? Then, by that stage, you are tired or have something else to do, and you still haven't started the large job? You may also have tried doing the large job first and getting it out of the way. Then the smaller jobs go by like a breeze, and you feel free at the end because you don't have that large job looming ahead of you anymore. Getting started on anything major in life can be like that.

So why not get it over and done with. Do what you have to do, and then it is out of the way. It will no longer haunt you and hang over you, making you feel bad because you still haven't done it yet.

If you spend your time thinking about niches and who will hire you and you don't know how to market and all those other things, you will destroy what little motivation you had in the beginning. These types of fears and thoughts are natural, and they explain why many of our grand plans and great ideas never materialize. We come up with so many problems and reasons why they won't work, so we give up.

## Your Training Is Underway

Let's suppose you have gotten as far as enrolling in a training program. Let's use the example of the home-study coaching kit because that's a popular one.

Maybe you even have some ideas of the niches in which you'd like to work. Maybe you have met other new coaches-in-training with whom you have plans to do some joint ventures. But when you sit down to listen to your tapes or CDs or read your manual, you freeze again, because that annoying little thought pops up again. You know, the one that goes like this: "This is such a huge undertaking. How am I ever going to get through this training program and find time to do the exam and actually do this! Have I bitten off more than I can chew?"

Do you hear the fear again? The negative self-talk? The lack of self-confidence? The self-sabotage?

Even when or if you have gotten so far as to bite the bullet and get the training you need, you are still coming up with reasons excusing you from doing it. And deep down inside is a sad part of you that recognizes this, and it makes you feel guilty and heavy-hearted because you know that getting the training is the only thing stopping you from achieving your dream. You are not looking ahead toward the final outcome, you are not in the present, and you are looking at all the hours of study in between and the exam at the end and doubting yourself again.

For some strange reason, you are imagining this study taking forever. In your mind, it's taking over your life. Many people feel this way when they first embark on adult-study courses. It is only natural to be concerned about time-management issues, but you must realize it isn't impossible, otherwise thousands of people around the world wouldn't be doing it right now!

When you worry about these types of things, those old doubts raise their heads again:

- I was lousy at school. How am I going to do this?
- People will know straight away that I'm not as smart as they are, and they'll be angry with me.
- I can't brag about a fancy education. Professional people won't want to hire me! I'm just wasting my time!
- I'll start this just as soon as I clean the attic!

You may be able to rationalize your fears at this point. You may be able to take yourself by the scruff of the neck and recognize silly fears when you see them. You know there is a niche out there for you, but the self-doubt and the negative self-talk is so ingrained in you because it has become a lifetime habit. Such habits are hard to shake!

## Why Let the Work Wait?

So here you are, ready to start yet unable to. You're sort of committed because you've invested the money in the program and, thus, your time. The fearful part of you wishes you'd never gotten in this deep already, whereas the rational part of you knows you are where you should be at this point in time. Part of you doesn't want to have wasted the money you have invested so far because that would really be foolish, but another part of you figures it would be best to just quit now before you get any further involved and waste any more time.

When you are in this situation, you need to reanalyze just what it is you are afraid of. Break down your study plan into small steps. At this stage, you are merely studying an interesting subject and even if you decide *not* to become a professional coach, the skills you will learn will help you with your relationships, your career, your children, and your spouse. Nothing you learn will be wasted. In fact, careerwise, just having studied and learned the skills will stand you in good stead. It will look very good on your resume. There, you don't feel quite so afraid now, do you?

If you are still cleaning your attic, washing your car, polishing your silver, and so on instead of studying, again, you need to ask yourself what it is you are afraid of. Why are you avoiding opening that training manual? If you are waiting for when you have more time, you may be waiting the rest of your life. The majority of us lead very full, busy lives. To make time to do anything more we have to find the time and rearrange our schedules to fit in extra things.

This can even happen *after* you have begun studying. When you hit a part that seems a bit challenging to you, again you will start thinking of cleaning the attic. It is only natural when we start something new that we start off all gung ho, full of energy and resolve, but some time into our new activity, we experience a drop-off of energy and excitement. The novelty wears off. We start questioning ourselves again. We begin to procrastinate—clean attics, wash cars, and polish silver!

Some things you do to avoid studying may be legitimate, and it may be important that you stop doing other things to complete them. But you need to look carefully at these situations and make sure that they are not just convenient excuses to avoid completing or continuing your studies.

Sure, polishing the silver is something you should do occasionally, but is it so important that you have to do it in your planned study time? You can always find excuses to do something else than study. That's how easy it is. That's how we sabotage ourselves. You may say, "My mother-in-law is visiting this weekend. She's fussy, so I *must* polish the silver right now!" Except, your mother-in-law has visited many times, and you've never worried about the silver before, so why, all of a sudden, are you worrying about it now? (If not to get out of studying!)

When in these situations, you need to remind yourself why you enrolled in the study program or bought the home-study kit in the first place. Sure, you can keep putting it off until you are 80 years old and can't focus on the print anymore. But that would be a waste of a very good study kit! And a waste of your life. Do you really want to put off the moment when you discover you really can earn a living as a coach, working from home, being your own boss, working your own hours, spending more time with your children, and so on? Ideally, you'd want that dream to happen as soon as possible, yes? If you create a sense of urgency around your studying, remember why it is important to you, you will find it easier to battle the urge to clean the attic!

## So Much to Do, So Little Time

A major hurdle for most people is prioritizing. So many things demand your immediate attention, there are so many distractions, so many things are important. How do you know where to begin? Your focus is scattered, and you find yourself running around like a headless chicken, not really achieving anything.

There are coaches who specialize in the niche of time management because you are not the only person on the planet who has this problem. In fact, you are just one of millions! Everyone from housewives, clerical workers, single parents, career women, CEOs, and anybody who is breathing, for that matter, has trouble prioritizing their lives so they get the most out of life and please themselves and their family and employers. Sounds like a lot to ask, and it is, but a trained coach knows how to do it. (Maybe that's a niche for you!)

"I don't have time" is such a common complaint these days. When a coach looks at the ways their clients spend their time, it is discovered that it is not that they don't have time, it is the way they spend the time they do have that is the problem.

No matter who you are, what you do, or where you live, you are always going to find life interrupted by distractions, planned or otherwise. Some of these distractions may even be created by yourself as part of your self-sabotage efforts.

Don't get us wrong, not all self-sought distractions are bad. There are times when you may be studying too much and you really should take a break. We all need a mental break now and then. All work and no play, remember? Sometimes a break can help us refocus on other activities with a fresh brain and improved performance. It's really only a problem when these distractions are commonplace and the reason you are permitting them to disrupt you is so you can avoid studying. Do you allow distractions to take you away from your study on a regular basis? Are those distractions important, or do you use them as excuses?

You can filter out unimportant distractions and choose not to let them disrupt you. Make the decision to be distracted only by those things that really cannot wait. These things are of an urgent nature. Choose not to be distracted by things that can wait. If you were cooking dinner or fixing a widget and somebody came to you wanting you to sharpen their pencil, chances are you'd say it can wait. When you are studying, these types of trivial distractions can wait, too. You must apply importance to your study and let others know of its importance and ask them not to interrupt you unless it is urgent.

If lack of motivation is affecting your study and you are looking for reasons to do anything else but study, recognize this is taking you away from your goal. The goal is to finish training and get out there and coach.

Every time you make an excuse to get out of studying or disrupt your studying, you are damaging your motivation. You are telling yourself your study is not as important as sharpening pencils or cleaning attics or whatever. You are telling yourself your dream of well-paid self-employment is not important. You are not important. Your life is not important. Your dreams are not important. Well, if you put it that way, just what are you doing on the planet wasting our oxygen!

Every excuse you make reduces your motivation. And it needn't be an important-sounding excuse either, it could be something like:

- I can't study now, I need to wait until I have lots of spare time with no interruptions.
- I'm not really in the mood now.
- Once such and such is finished, then I will really be able to focus on studying.
- When I win the Lotto, I'll be able to study when I like.
- When the kids complete this year at school, then they'll be older and then I'll be able to study.
- Once the attic is cleaned, then I'll be able to study. Except, maybe I should do something about the garage, too, while I'm at it!

All your excuses are just reasons to avoid returning to your studies. The more excuses you make and use to disrupt you, the less motivated you feel and the harder it becomes.

## Your Exam Is Approaching

Don't be fooled into thinking that self-sabotage can't affect you if you are near the end. You may have just one last chapter to study or one last class to listen to on CD, and it can strike.

Why would it strike now? Maybe you realize that now you are so close to the moment of truth: the exam, the certification, and taking your newfound skills out into the big wide world! Your fears set in. Are you ready? Are you good enough? Smart enough? Can you really do it?

If you don't finish your study, then you are safe, because you are never going to be put into the position to find out if you're really going to be able to pull it off.

Maybe you find new ways to procrastinate. Maybe your attic is so clean—and your house, your car, and your silver—that you've run out of things to clean. So now you start thinking, "Have I really absorbed everything? Am I ready for the exam? Maybe I'd just better go back and restudy Chapters X and Y again."

Going back and restudying is not a bad idea if you really believe it will help you, but if you are doing it merely to avoid completing your studies, then you have a problem: self-sabotage.

What is it you are really afraid of?

- If I fail the exam, everyone will think I'm a loser and laugh at me!
- Not succeeding now will just confirm that I'm not good enough. Who wants proof of that!
- I can continue to *pretend* if things stay as they are, but I won't be able to pretend if I'm slapped with the reality that I'm a failure.

Whoa! Stop right there! If you sit and don't pass the coaching exam on the first try, how does this make you a failure? Do you know that there are many well-known, very successful coaches in the world who had to sit their exam more than once? Honestly! And it's not because the exam is difficult—it isn't. In fact, one of Terri's assistants asked her once, "Why do you give 14 days to do this exam?

It could be done in a few hours!" Yes, it could be done in a few hours, and some people do it in a few hours. But some people also have busy careers and families to look after, and for them, being able to spread out their exam is a blessing.

So, now you know you can dispel the visions you have kept from your school exam days, knowing that sitting your coaching exam is not like that. Whew!

But you may be still worried about what if you fail!

For a start, if you do not pass the first time round, we do not call you a failure! In fact, at the Coaching Institute (http://www.coachinstitute .com), if you do not pass the first time, the examiners tell you what aspect of your exam stopped you from succeeding. This allows you to go back and practice that part again so that you can resit the examination knowing that the one thing that held you back the first time has now been conquered!

It's not like when you were at school and received your exam back with nothing but a low score on it, and you were left wondering where you went wrong and why you didn't pass. At the Coaching Institute, they tell you exactly why you didn't pass, so you can work on it and try again.

Or maybe you are hesitant to show the world what you're made of. This comes back to lack of self-confidence, self-doubt, and fear — self-sabotage! Many people are afraid of being themselves and showing their true self for fear of being ridiculed or laughed at.

Fear of failure holds many people back. Maybe it is holding you back. Again you think, "It's better not to try and then fail and make a fool of myself. So I just won't try."

Or maybe you are thinking, "What if I succeed and pass! What if I get my coaching certification! Then I'll be expected to actually go out there and market myself and get real clients! What a horrifying thought!"

You know, sometimes people are just as afraid of success as they are of failure, for these very reasons.

Although it is desirable that you take your studies seriously and place importance on your studies, it is not healthy to build this up into such a big thing that you start to become stressed about it. Becoming a coach is not the be-all and end-all of your existence. Nobody said you have to become an overnight success. Nobody said you have to have X number of clients in the first month or you're doomed. Nobody said you had to give up your day job. Many people choose to coach part-time, when it suits them. It's fun and it's pocket money. Many coaches do find they eventually build such a large client database that the decision then becomes one of "Well, is now the time to quit my day job? Something has to go because I can no longer do both."

If you experience any of these fears, we hope you realize now that there is nothing to be worried about. What you are imagining is worse than the reality. When you allow your fears to invade your thinking to this extent, you are more likely to increase your negative self-talk. You'll be predicting your failure and expecting it! The fearful thoughts we have are unlikely to be rational, so unless we have some form of evidence to support a fear, we shouldn't give it too much power.

Another form of self-sabotage at this stage of the proceedings is when you go the opposite way and avoid completing your studies or taking the exam because you have now convinced yourself that you don't have to do it. This can be very comforting for a short while, until you start to feel guilty about all the money and time you have invested and how it will all go to waste.

You can hold yourself back by saying things like, "I've finished and I've just got the exam to do, so I don't have to do that straight away. I can do that later." Or maybe you think, "To give myself every chance, maybe I should go back and study the entire course again!" Or you may even be thinking, "Gee, while I was studying, the attic got awfully dusty, so maybe I had better do that first."

Of course, you don't *have* to do it! You don't *have* to do anything you don't want to do. But why did you start in the first place? Remember your goal. You want to be successful on your own terms, be your own boss, work your own hours, be able to spend more time at home with your family, and so on. And having a coaching practice sure beats selling Avon for a living. You don't have to knock on doors or rely on the sale of products to make a few peanuts. Coaches earn a lot more than any Avon lady we've ever known. (Not that there is anything wrong with Avon or its sales representatives! We just wish to point out there are easier ways to make more money.)

You chose coaching because it is a self-employed occupation that is respectable, enjoyable, and fun and that will enable you to have the type of freedom you cannot have working for someone else. You may also have chosen it not only for these reasons but also because you can earn a great deal of money from this profession.

Maybe you can't complete the exam because you don't think you are ready. If you have studied according to the guidelines and used the resources to help you, you should not be worried about your level of readiness—unless you are a perfectionist. Perfectionists always put off finishing things because they don't believe it is perfect enough yet.

You can waste your time going over and over your study materials if you already know them. Even when you sit your written exam, you can probably find many different ways to answer one question. Your answer doesn't have to be perfect; it just has to be right.

If you have come as far as the exam and find you can't complete it because you don't believe your answers are perfect, you can waste valuable time making irrelevant changes that don't alter the correctness of the answer and serve little purpose other than to please your perfectionism. You can spend your entire two weeks trying to perfect your exam answers only to discover you've missed the deadline and have to resit a new exam and pay a resitting fee!

Do you see how your thinking can sabotage your efforts and your goals?

Fortunately, coach training is fun and interesting. It is bringing you one step closer to the career of your dreams. Remember this and get studying to get your coaching career on track!

# 6

# Focused on Your Goal

*If you chase two rabbits, both will escape.*

— Anonymous

Becoming highly successful in coaching, or any other field for that matter, requires a high level of focus. You've surely heard stories of how the best entrepreneurs say that the one thing that helped them succeed is remaining highly focused on their goals.

## Focused on Your Vision

The focus that you need is of two sorts. The first is a general vision, which we have discussed. The vision is the fishbowl idea. Your coaching business is the fish, and your vision is the bowl. How big will your fish/business grow? To the size of your bowl. A big bowl is a big vision. Keeping this ultimate vision in focus will help you get there.

One of the best ways to stay focused on your vision is to create a mission that is directly in line with your vision. Do you have a mission for your coaching business? You probably do, even if you have not written it down or articulated it. It would be almost impossible to be in the coaching world and not have your mission include something about helping others achieve their goals and dreams. Once you have your vision and mission, you can create specific objectives. The objectives are your methods for achieving the mission. This brings us to the second type of focus, which has to do with daily implementation.

Throughout this chapter we will help you achieve the day-to-day focus necessary for turning your dream into reality. We will tackle all of those things that can keep you from remaining focused.

## Identify What Distracts You

Most coaches work from home-based offices. Because coaching is typically over the telephone, it often does not make sense to rent an office if you can coach from a home office. After working with dozens of home-based business owners, including coaches and owners of other industries, it is clear to us that one of the biggest challenges is that of becoming distracted.

You may not become distracted during your actual coaching calls, but what about during all of your other activities. Do you ever become distracted while doing things like working on your web site copy, creating your marketing materials, creating products, setting up meetings with referral partners, and reading and educating yourself?

### *Understanding the Source of Distraction*

- Do you know what accounts for the majority of your distractions?
- Do you know specifically what types of activities best hold your focus and attention?
- Do you know what gets you off track and what gets you back on track?

If you don't, then it is time to find out. You need to know how your attention works and what interferes with it, what works to get you refocused, and so on.

You want to be particularly aware of whether you are primarily distracted by internal stimuli or external stimuli. Here's the difference:

An *internal stimulus* can be:

- A thought.
- A fear or worry.
- A sense of hunger or thirst.
- A physical pain or discomfort.

- A feeling of tiredness or fatigue.
- A lack of energy.
- A sense of restlessness.
- A lack of interest in what you are doing.
- A frustration or irritation.
- A sense of guilt (that you should be doing something else).
- A sense of boredom or dissatisfaction with what you are doing.
- A lack of ideas.

Some *external or environmental stimuli* can be:

- The phone ringing.
- Your husband, wife, or partner asking you a question.
- A television or radio program.
- People talking nearby.
- A computer screen pop-up or your e-mail.
- A colleague knocking on your door or interrupting you.
- Your child asking you to play.
- A book sitting on your desk that looks interesting.
- A smell in the room where you are working.
- A too-hot or too-cold environment.

### *The Whys of Attention Wandering*

It is also important to identify whether you get distracted on purpose. You may actually choose to get distracted because you want a mental break or you want to look something up on the Internet or because you are bored.

You can tell that you are distracted on purpose when there is a conscious thought component to your distraction. You tell yourself, "I'm going to take a break for a minute to look up the weather forecast for tomorrow." Or "My hands are really getting tired from typing, so I'm going to go for a quick walk around the block." Sometimes effortful distraction is a smart thing. Other times it serves as an excuse.

Many people who struggle to maintain their focus say that they get distracted without realizing it. "All of a sudden, I realized that I was in the midst of thinking about something totally unrelated to my marketing plan." Or "I didn't realize that I was surfing the web and not working on my project until about five minutes later." Or "I thought I was paying attention to what I was reading only to learn that I had read 10 pages and remembered nothing."

Record all of the things that distract you over a four-day time period. Use a form that looks something like this:

| Situation | Distraction | Internal/ External | Purposeful |
|---|---|---|---|
| Working on my marketing plan | Thinking about how no one would buy it or like it | Internal | No |
| Tired after writing | Looked at a web site and decided to shop online for 15 minutes | External | Yes |

## Strategies to Improve Focus

Monitoring your attention is the first step to improving your ability to focus and attend to information over an extended period of time. Once you know what types of things distract you in an unhelpful way, you can work on changing them.

### *Postpone Internal Distractions*

If you noticed that you tend to get distracted by internal factors (thoughts, mind wandering, internal sensations, etc.), then you can start to train yourself to recognize them.

You can say, "Oh, wait a minute, I am now thinking about what my marketing mentor will say about my plan when what I am supposed to be doing is researching ideas."

The more you practice identifying your internal distractions, the more quickly you will begin to be able to catch them. The good thing about dealing with distractions is once you catch them, you can quickly change the situation and get yourself back on track.

Once you have identified a thought or other internal distraction that is keeping you from remaining focused, you can decide to delay the distraction. With the previous example (thinking and worrying about your marketing plan while you are researching), you can tell yourself, "I will continue researching for another 30 minutes and then switch gears to work on my marketing plan."

Don't try to ignore your internal distractions or try to push them away because they will keep coming back, perhaps more often or more strongly. Instead, tell yourself that you will deal with the thoughts or feelings that are capturing your attention. If what distracts you is a fearful thought or self-doubt, then the best thing to do is to write down the thought that goes through your mind. Then try to go back to what you were doing. Come back to that distracting thought once you have finished your task. Don't worry, these things will still be there; you can come back to them!

If the thought continues to bother you for some time, take a break and deal with it right then. Handle it in the manner described in Chapter 4, in which you weigh the evidence on both sides and think about the concern in a different way.

If you consistently do this, then your internal distractions will decrease over time. On the other hand, if you continue to respond to these thoughts and concerns that distract you, you will have more distracting thoughts. Teach these thoughts that it is not okay to interrupt you when you are busy and focused. Your goal is to achieve that laser-beam focus.

This is where mental training comes in. You are training your mind to focus and concentrate on tasks for indefinite lengths of time. You will ultimately be deterred by nothing as you work toward your goal.

In summary, the best way to deal with internal distractions:

1. First, acknowledge the thought that is distracting you. Make yourself aware of it by making a mental note or writing it down.
2. Second, decide not to let that thought interfere with your concentration. Do not actively try to push the thought away because it will fight back. Instead, let it roll off you like water off a duck's back.

3. Third, plan to come back to the thoughts at a later period of time when you can focus your energy productively on them.
4. Fourth, immediately redirect your mental energy toward the task you are concentrating on.

### *Filter out External Distractions*

You have two options for handling external distractions:

1. The first is to control your environment so that these types of interruptions are reduced.
2. The second is to learn how to tune out external distractions.

In psychology, the strategy of changing your environment to improve your performance or reduce temptations that will bring you off track is called *stimulus control.* This is an effective strategy that works for many situations, such as weight loss, anger management, and substance abuse. It can also help you improve your attention.

Basically, the idea is to remove distracting objects from your environment. Well, that makes perfect sense, doesn't it?!

For example, some people become distracted from what they are doing by checking their e-mail. Sound familiar? They may not consciously think, "Oh, now it's time to check my e-mail"—many programs put a flashing icon on your computer task bar to alert you to incoming mail—and for many of us, that is all we need to be distracted. You try to focus on what's on your screen—the task at hand—and out of the corner of your eye you see that little flashing icon. It can drive you crazy. Most programs give you the option of turning that off, so if this is a distraction for you, turn it off! But we digress. . . . With or without that annoying flashing icon telling you "You've got mail!" most people rationalize that because checking their e-mail is work-related, it is therefore a worthwhile activity. Well, yes, it is, but you don't need to check your e-mail every 10 minutes when you are trying to work on something. You can check your e-mail every hour. Some people only check it once or twice a day—imagine that! Being disturbed by incoming e-mail and feeling the need to check it will interrupt your concentration and focus and keep you from achieving whatever it is you are doing.

So, for stimulus control, you can close your e-mail program and open it only when it is appropriate to check your e-mails or work off-line. Or, as suggested previously, turn off any sounds or visual aids, like flashing icons in the task bar, that will distract you.

Out of sight, out of mind!

Another business- and work-related distraction is a ringing telephone. Take it off the hook. Turn off your phone. If you are really worried about missing calls, use a voice-message service or answering machine.

What are some more distractions? Comfort can be one. If you find that your work environment is too warm and it makes you feel sleepy, then turn down the heat. If you are too cold, turn the heat up or put on some warm clothes.

If other people disrupt your work, schedule specific times when it will be less likely that you will be interrupted. This might be very early in the morning or late in the evening. Also, let the people in your life know that during these specific times, you want to be interrupted only if something is truly an emergency, and you'd best define what constitutes an emergency. People's ideas of emergencies can differ!

You need to be aware of all the little things in your environment that distract you. Some of them might be quite subtle. You might like to keep a notebook and jot down each time you identify a distraction so you can do something about it.

For example, if your dog walking up and down the hall near your office is distracting, arrange to have the dog in a different part of the house while you are working. If the custodian's vacuuming distracts you, plan not to work at the time when the vacuum will be running.

Another important aspect in your environment is the *optimal noise level*. People really are different when it comes to this particular distraction. For some, it isn't a distraction at all, but a necessity.

Some people are much better able to stay focused when they have background noise. For these people, a quiet room is distracting, and some form of noise helps them stay focused. (If you have a teenager who insists he can do his homework with the TV on, watch him. He may be telling you the truth!) There is some evidence that people with mild attention difficulties do better when there is a greater level of audible stimulation, because filtering out other, perhaps smaller, annoying noises can help you stay focused on your task at hand.

One of Terri Levine's assistants finds that she does her best work when there is *specific* external noise. When she sits in a quiet room and tries to work, she becomes distracted by her own thought processes or by all the silly noises that she can hear: crickets outside, a car door closing across the road, a siren in the distance, a buzzing fly, the dog snoring. And she is also more likely to create distractions for herself, like looking at her e-mail.

On the other hand, when she has the TV on or a CD playing, she finds that because she must concentrate all her mental energy on the task at hand, it is easier to do so. Her mind does not wander in the same way it does in a quiet environment.

Larina Kase admits she is this way as well. In college and graduate school, she had difficulty concentrating when in a quiet library. She could do her best studying in a noisy café. She is still this way. Now she works with a television or radio on. She brings a book to a coffee shop and enjoys reading in a busy atmosphere.

So you see, the way that people focus their attention is highly individualized. Some need absolute silence, some like a little noise, some like to work in a rock concert. Any option is perfect for you as long as it works for you. Interestingly, many babies who are problem sleepers, sleep very well when the vacuum cleaner is running!

Do not deny your natural style — go with it. If you know that you work well with noise, then find out what type of noise works best for you. White noise such as a fan, a clothes dryer, or a noise machine may be the best because there are no specific sounds to distract you as there would be listening to music. Other people work great with a television or radio on in the background. Try different environments to see which works best for you, and don't be surprised if your mind changes occasionally. One day you might find you concentrate better if there is no noise even if most of the time you prefer the TV or radio on in the background.

Don't kid yourself, though, and be honest. If you do like the TV on while you work, is it really because you find it helps you concentrate or because having it on lets you watch your favorite programs while you work. (Or try to work!) If you suspect it is the latter, why not make a deal with yourself. Say you'll finish your work first and then watch some TV. Use the TV as a reward.

Of course, there are going to be times when some people cannot do anything about the environment in which they work. They just have to live with certain distracting activities or sounds around them. So, if you cannot change your environment, you need to learn how to focus despite the distractions. Although this takes considerable practice, it is something you can learn to do.

It's a matter of training again. You can practice by working despite the distractions. You begin by working on something that is very engaging and enjoyable because any external distraction is not quite as likely to put you off. Then try working on a more mundane activity in the same distracting environment. You can find lots of places to practice this technique. You can go to a café and try to work with your laptop or go to a busy park or work with your television or radio turned up. These situations give you the opportunity to train yourself to be able to focus despite the distraction.

## Schedule Distractions

Of course, not all distractions are bad or negative. Used in certain ways, breaks in your attention can be useful. No one can maintain solid attention indefinitely, and sometimes taking a break can actually help you refocus. Maybe you've noticed when your thoughts become muddled and you've been looking at something for too long, taking a break from it has enabled you to return to the task with fresh eyes and renewed focus.

Also, knowing that you have a planned break coming up can help you stay motivated and focused as you work on your marketing plan. For example, if you tell yourself you have to work on your marketing plan for, say, three straight hours, you may become distracted and lose motivation because you just can't stay focused for three straight hours on that particular project. You may then develop a negative association to working on your project. This type of association is not helpful at all.

On the other hand, if you tell yourself that you will work on it for, say, one hour and then take a coffee break and sit outside or read the paper, then work on it for another hour or so, the task is not so daunting or tiring, and you will be able to remain focused.

If you want to help yourself stay focused on something—marketing your business, for example—reward yourself when you actually do so. If you reward yourself with scheduled breaks, not only will this assist you to stay focused but it will increase the likelihood that you will continue to work on the task.

## Should I Multitask?

*The shorter way to do many things is to do only one thing at a time.*
— Mozart

We know many people think of multitasking as a positive thing, but when you are working on a serious project, such as marketing your business, the answer is usually, no. Don't multitask. Working on your business is not like cleaning a house, in which it doesn't really matter in what order you clean the house or which cleaning activities you do first or simultaneously.

On the other hand, it is a good idea to multitask with unimportant activities because you can get lots of things accomplished quickly; just don't do it with the important stuff. If you try multitasking while you are working on your marketing project, you're telling yourself that your project is not really an important task. You don't want to give your mind that idea!

Your marketing plan, for example, needs to be an important task, and it deserves your focus and 100 percent attention.

With multitasking, you simply cannot pay 100 percent attention to any one of the things you are doing. It's like juggling. There is no way that you can pay attention to any one of three balls because you will drop the other two, and this is why you don't want to multitask with important tasks.

This is when scheduling becomes important. With important projects, schedule time to focus 100 percent on that one task, and when that is finished, you can move on to the next.

Unless you are a skilled juggler and someone who has a natural ability for multitasking, don't try to multitask when you are working on your marketing project. This is extra important if you struggle with issues like time management in the first place and are not somebody who can do many things at once.

## Breaking Up and Prioritizing Tasks

If you are in the position of having many things on your plate, you probably already know the importance of prioritizing your activities.

Secretaries and personal assistants must be good at juggling many activities at once, for example. Working mothers must be adept jugglers, too, as must single parents. You have constant demands on your time and constant activities competing for your limited time and attention. It can be stressful, and because you have so much to accomplish, you can't afford to ignore the rest while you focus on just one thing. You have to do it all and do it well.

By prioritizing your activities, you will make decisions more quickly and stay more focused. You won't waste time deciding whether you will do something and when you will or should do it. You will know that only a legitimate emergency will interfere with your prioritized activities. You will not be distracted by the thought of other activities awaiting your attention either, because you have already scheduled them.

Here are some questions to ask yourself in determining your list of top priorities:

- *Is this task very significant and meaningful to me?*
- *Will I feel a significant sense of accomplishment if I work on this?*
- *Is there a time deadline for this activity (either an outside deadline or a self-imposed one)?*
- *Would other people stand to benefit from my completing this project?*
- *If I were not able to work on this, would there be some negative consequences?*
- *Could I miss an important opportunity if I did not do this now?*
- *Would doing or not doing this set a precedent for other activities in my life?*

Prioritizing tasks helps you determine the order in which you should work on them. Once you know the order of your projects, if your priority task is very large, consider breaking it into a series of smaller tasks. This idea is very useful for people who have attention difficulties, and here's why.

Large tasks take a long time to complete. If you have the attention span of a flea, your mind will very likely jump onto something else and become distracted before you complete the task. So, instead, break down your large project into several steps that you will follow in order to finish the task. Remember to schedule small breaks in between these steps to regain your focus and keep you motivated.

Write down the steps of your project and then check them off as you go. This process can motivate you and make the steps that you need to get done very clear. You won't get lost or confused or forget anything. You will know exactly what you need to get done and when. You will remain on track.

Okay. Now you are set to work on your coaching business and marketing plan, yes? But where's your motivation to actually do it? Are you thinking of cleaning the attic again? Well, let's look at that next.

# 7

# The Power of Self-Motivation

*If we don't discipline ourselves, the world will do it for us.*
— William Feather

Are you truly motivated to build your coaching business? How do you know this? Could you be more motivated? Are the right things motivating you? Let's take a look at these ideas.

## Understand Your Motivation

All of us have activities that fuel our passion and motivation. We do these things easily and have no problem with distractions. We also have other activities that drain our motivation, that we may not particularly enjoy doing, and we become easily distracted. In fact, with those types of activities we may even look forward to distractions so as to avoid doing them. Children do this when you ask them to clean their rooms!

Of course, it is easy to understand why doing something we love and enjoy motivates us to do it. We don't even need motivating to do these things. Once we do something that we feel we must do but would rather not do, however, we become unmotivated. We lose interest. We may feel we're losing our energy, too. We feel sapped and drained. Some of these types of activities are not obvious to us, but once you start to observe your energy level, you will start to learn which activities drain your energy and which build your energy and enthusiasm.

It is a good idea, when possible, to schedule those activities that drain your energy at times of the day when you are naturally alert and energetic.

### *Energy as a Clue to Motivation*

Energy is often a direct reflection of motivation. As an example, think of a time when you have felt tired and disinterested, but then you may have received some exciting news, and suddenly you felt awake and reenergized. And it works the other way, too. Maybe you were full of energy and enthusiasm and then received some bad news, and suddenly you felt drained and tired.

Take note of when you are feeling motivated, energized, interested, courageous, creative, and animated. What was going on at those times? What were you thinking about or doing?

Then record those times when you feel uninspired, bored, unimaginative, bland, fatigued, tired, or restless. What thoughts or behaviors led to you experiencing these feelings? What specifically drained your energy?

Read your energy. It has a lot to tell you, and the answers will help you schedule your tasks in ways that will enable you to accomplish the most in the easiest manner.

Some people experience the most energy at a particular time of day—either in the morning or in the evening. We have what we call morning people and night owls. Example: One client, let's call him Fred, felt most energized in the early evenings and the least energy in midmorning. He was a financial advisor and was beginning to work on a new entrepreneurial business venture. He was not yet 100 percent sure that he really wanted to do this entrepreneurial venture because it had certain elements of risk with which he was not yet entirely comfortable.

In reading Fred's energy to get a sense of what truly inspired and motivated him, it was discovered that he was doing his research and working on his marketing campaign on his computer in the mornings. Remember that morning is the time of day when he naturally feels unenergized, unmotivated and easily bored. So he wasn't getting much done.

And guess what he was doing in the evenings? He was thinking about his business idea and talking with colleagues about getting it going. He was gathering information and writing a business plan — fun stuff that was rewarding and enjoyable.

Knowing what you know now, you can probably figure out what was happening here and what changes he needed to make. He needed to do the things that are naturally motivating in the morning when his energy is naturally lowest and do the things that are more challenging and effortful in the evenings when he has greater amounts of energy and motivation.

### Personality and Circumstance for Energy

There are other variables at play when it comes to figuring out your energy. There are several physiological variables that can impact on your energy, and these are divided into state and trait variables.

A *trait variable* is a constant for you. Evidence exists that people are more awake and energized at certain times of the day. We remind you again of the idea of a person being classified a morning person or night person, which has scientific validity. It has to do with your body temperature rising and falling naturally. If you tend to be most energetic in the late afternoon and evening, then you may be more of a night person, and maybe you even call yourself a night owl.

A *state variable* is one that changes because it is influenced by certain conditions. If you have a cup of coffee every afternoon at 4 p.m. and feel most energized by 4:30 p.m., then a state variable may be at play. It is the caffeine energizing you; you are not naturally energized at that time of the day.

Take note of the impact that food, water, sugary beverages, caffeine, and alcohol have on you. Other state variables include things like your mood on a given day, things having to do with relationships, and your progress with your business. You are going to be much more cheerful and energetic when you have received good news and things are going well.

In Fred's case, he did turn out to be a natural night person, which is part of the reason that he was most energized in the evenings and felt sluggish in the mornings.

To see if this was the main factor at play, he moved his schedule around for a few weeks, trying different activities at certain times of the day. He consistently found that his energy was higher when he was involved with action-oriented entrepreneurial pursuits in which he interacted with others than when he was involved with planning, research, and writing activities. For Fred to attain maximum productivity then, he should schedule the least-motivating tasks for those times when his energy and concentration levels are naturally high. It will help him get through it.

We were also able to use Fred's personality to help create maximum motivation. He is an extrovert, so we wanted to use that to his advantage. By definition, being extroverted means that you glean energy from being around others. He ended up scheduling morning meetings with people because he has less energy then and gained energy by being around other people. He was then able to use his whole day productively, and the situation was win-win.

## The Stages of Motivation

A lack of motivation is very often associated with ambivalent feelings:

- "I really want to create this marketing plan, *but . . .* "
- "If only I knew I had a good market, then I would be highly motivated to do this project."

You may have experienced this yourself. Part of you really wants to do your marketing project, yet part of you is not 100 percent sure. This indecisiveness is why you experience inner struggle and conflict and lack motivation. You don't feel you can totally write off the project because it has potential and you want to do it, but you don't feel ready yet to commit yourself to it. It's a dilemma.

Resolving ambivalence is the key to creating a change in your life. The research of William R. Miller, Ph.D., and Stephen Rollnick, Ph.D. (2002), provides keys toward how to motivate others and ourselves. Prochaska and DiClemente created a process model, which indicates that there are specific stages of change that we go through. These bodies of research and theory were born out of work with substance abusers, but have been expanded to apply to many aspects of life, motivation, and change.

We often assume that we are ready to change; however, just because something sounds like an important idea, it does not mean that we are *ready* to do it.

It is important to figure out which stage of motivation you are currently in. Once you know that, you can propel yourself forward to the next stage. You can do this more easily and swiftly if you engage the services of a professional coach.

Of course, one of the best ways to propel your motivation forward is to create success that energizes you to keep moving ahead. Knowing where her clients are in terms of motivation has been one of the secrets to the success of Terri Levine's work as a coach. Some coaches make the inaccurate assumption that their clients are ready to spring into action, but this may not always be the case. As you read through the types of readiness for change stages outlined in the following paragraphs, think of them for yourself and also for your clients. The best way to learn how to use something with your clients is to learn it yourself first.

Here are Miller and Rollnick's stages as put forth in their theory of motivational interviewing:

1. **Precontemplation.** In this stage, you are not yet thinking about making a change. Perhaps this is because you have not thought about doing something new or because you have already thought things through and decided not to make a change. It doesn't mean that you do not want to change; it could be that you do not feel that you could successfully make the change.

   If you are in this stage, it may not be a good idea to try to force yourself to start the serious work on your marketing project. Instead, this is the time to gather information about marketing your business or working with a consultant who can help you. Or it may be a good time to do nothing and put your project on hold for a bit until you are sure. It is a much better idea to begin something when you are *ready* to make a change rather than try to push yourself into it and experience failure.

2. **Contemplation.** At this stage, you have probably begun to think about changing but are not sure about what to do. You think of the pros and cons, and it can be a time of confusion. You want to begin working on it, but you also don't want to begin work on it. When you are in this stage, you may want to make a for-and-against list for doing or not doing your project. Use this list to help you decide whether to go ahead toward the next stage or take some more time to think about it.

3. **Preparation.** This stage appears when you feel that the reasons to change outweigh the reasons not to change, and you feel determined to do something. You start thinking about how you can make the change, and you feel more ready within yourself to do something new. Determined or otherwise, however, in this stage, you are still not quite ready for action, but you are getting close.

   You might like to commence by doing small things, like preparatory work. For example, during this stage you might look at how to set up a web site or gather information about how to market your business online. It's doing your homework. At this stage, you will probably feel ready to change within the next month.

4. **Action.** As the name implies, this is the action stage, and you are now ready to go ahead and implement your change plans. It's at about this point that you may start telling others about your plans. Now is the right time to push yourself because you are mentally and physically ready to make serious progress on your project. If you are experiencing ambivalence or decreased energy related to your new project, you may still be in an earlier stage and not quite ready for action. It is not uncommon to fluctuate between two stages, especially two that are next to each other, like preparation and action.

5. **Maintenance.** You enter this stage once you have been successful in implementing (and keeping) the changes. You will try to sustain the progress you've made and not return to your old habits! Having said that, it is not uncommon to slip occasionally and find the old avoidance or procrastination issues rise up. This won't be a serious problem as long as you are aware it is happening, take steps to overcome it, and continue to make progress. The most important part of this stage is that you recognize what you need to do next and motivate yourself to keep up progress.

Going back to our friend, Fred. He was in the preparation stage and not yet ready to commit to take action, but he was ready to begin planning for a career change, and at his level he was able to gather information and begin networking with contacts. If Terri, as his coach, had pushed him into the action stage, when he wasn't 100 percent ready, he would have felt pressured and unprepared and may not have been successful. People should not be pushed beyond their current stage unless they are ready for it.

### Interview with Sharon Wilson

Cofounder of the Coaching Institute (http://www.coach institute.com) and CEO of Coaching from Spirit.com (http://www.coachingfromspirit.com).

**Can you tell the readers about your work as a coach?**
I have the great honor of being the founder and chief spiritual officer of Coaching from Spirit.com and also cofounder of the Coaching Institute with Terri Levine. I have coauthored several books, including *Intentional Change* (Cape Elizabeth, ME: Xlibris Corporation, 1999), *Living an Extraordinary Life* (Buckingham, PA: Lahaska Press, 2001), *Coaching with Spirit* (San Francisco: Jossey-Bass Pfeiffer, 2002). These books explore the new paradigms of coaching that are emerging, which focus on personal growth and expanded consciousness, and I see this happening everywhere! People are waking up to the possibilities of how this world can be if we all join together in thought, word, feeling, and action! People are beginning to see that there is more to us all than what we can physically experience with our five senses.

I have coached hundreds of professionals, executives, entrepreneurs, coaches, and everything in between! This is the shift that is happening! "Normal" people activating their natural abilities to have two-way communications with the Divine (whatever they choose to call it) Source and remembering that they are cocreators in this life experience. Through this awakening of their two-way connection they are practically implementing these Universal Laws of Energy to *create new realities:* a world of love, joy, peace, and prosperity!

I work with individuals on real-life issues and offer my clients techniques and tools to bridge the inner and outer worlds in effective ways. Spiritual coaching focuses on helping you make

*(continued)*

79

inner shifts in energy focus and perceptions to attract, more easily, what you desire in your life! Simply put, I help my clients and the coaches I mentor create new realities!

**You offer great support for coaches. What are some of the products and services?**
At Coaching from Spirit we recently completed two home-study kits called 30 Days to Creating Success from the Inside Out! and How to Use Spiritual Business Building Skills to Create the Business of Your Dreams! They can be used both for coaches to their clients in a spiritual approach to accomplishing their goals.

We also offer a teleseminar coaching program called the Empowered Spiritual Coach that shows you how to activate spiritual coaching skills in yourself and in your clients to help them more easily tap into laws of attraction and to make changes at an inner level in their beliefs, patterns, and behaviors, so they can take the actions that will allow them to create more of what they want.

**What are some great ways you have seen coaches create inspiration and motivation for themselves?**
I have been so blessed to be able to mentor so many coaches and help them create the life and businesses they want. I am so impressed with the type of people that are attracted to the profession of coaching. They are focused on the intention of serving others and making a positive impact in this world. I have seen coaches create inspiration by focusing not on how to change others so that their reality changes but to instead focus on how they can change themselves!

I see coaches every day that inspire and motivate others by walking their talk and coming from an intention to see the good in others and focus on what is working instead of what is not working. So much is going right in each of our lives!

But we can tend to first look at what has not happened *yet*. I see coaches committed to seeing what is working, and as they do that, more works! I am so honored to be part of a profession that I believe has as its primary intention to activate the possibilities in ourselves and in turn in each other! I am also touched when

I see coaches giving of themselves to help another coach who needs someone to see them as they want to be seen.

For example, one coach I mentor holds a telegathering every week to help other coaches magnetize clients by the group holding the intention of the perfect clients who are called to them to find them in joyful ways. First they visualize this for themselves, then they expand that vision to see everyone in the world more prosperous. People leave feeling expanded, and they can feel the energy they sent out coming back to them. It is a powerful way to start their day!

### What blocks motivation to develop as a coach and build a successful coaching business?

One thing: your own beliefs! It is so important as a coach to really get clear on what are the beliefs you hold about developing as a coach. For example, when you think about attracting clients, does it feel hard? What are the thoughts that come to you as you think of that subject? I suggest each coach create a vision of their ideal life and business—really get into the feelings of it. Then let yourself notice any of the thoughts that come up. I call those the "yeah buts." Yeah that would be nice, but how could I ever do that? Who will ever pay me that much?

As you look at the yeah buts, you will see the thoughts that have become a pattern for you, and you can begin to take baby steps to create a new pattern. Beliefs are just thoughts we have thought over and over until they become like a well-worn path. To create a new belief, we have to make small changes in those patterns. They can't change overnight.

So, to simply start noticing the patterns is the first step toward creating new ones. I also think most coaches don't feel good about the idea of selling their services, and so in turn when they are talking to people, people feel their energy of that belief. I believe that selling is serving and that when someone has something that can serve us there is a vibrational matching that occurs. So it is like you are an answer to their prayer and they are an answer to yours!

*(continued)*

For coaches to do well, they need to develop a selling process that fits for them and feels good for them. I also believe that you are never alone, and as a coach you are not building your business alone. You have angels and guides . . . fairies of the universe . . . call it what you will, but you have guidance that is helping you—you just have to ask—you have to connect daily with that inner guidance and let that guidance help you. By focusing on the intention of how you want to feel as you build your business, you will then be guided to the actions to take that are a match to that feeling . . . that essence . . . and you will become magnetic to people who are in alignment with your intentions.

**How can coaches use spirit or motivation to create top-quality coaching services and products?**
By allowing themselves to tap into that higher guidance in everything they do. Start with the intention that you are not doing this alone and ask for the highest guidance to help you. Focus on how you want to feel as you create the product or service. I suggest coaches create what I call an order to the universe.

Before you do anything, get clear first on what you don't want in the experience and what you don't want to feel. That helps you surface it all up. It is there under the surface anyway! Next, focus on how you want to feel as you put this together or build this business.

Write it all out and *feel* the feelings; as you do, you will activate the passion! Then start to create the actions that are in alignment with that passion. Take baby steps if you need to but *take action.*

That action will create momentum, and things will come to you in amazing ways. You will be connected with the exact perfect people who can help you. Doors will open for you. As you go through your day, look for what is working and jot it down in your appreciation journal or positive-evidence journal. You are changing what you are attracting by how you are focusing your attention!

You will be amazed at how things will work out even when you don't have any idea on how it could all work out. Stay focused on looking for the good in all things and you will attract more of that.

## Inspiration for Motivation

It's easy to be motivated when you feel inspired. Your energy and enthusiasm are plentiful when you are doing something you love and feel passionate about.

Keep this in mind when you are selecting your coaching or marketing niche. Don't just pick a niche because you think there's a bigger market for it. If the niche doesn't inspire you, you won't be as successful in it and it will seem like hard work. Choose something that feels right, and the rest will follow naturally. You need to believe in the path you choose for yourself.

In a nutshell, if you want to remain energized, enthusiastic, and feel motivated to work on your business plan or write your marketing plan, you need to believe in it. You need to feel that the *value* of your service or product is so great that the product can sell itself.

Of course, we know it is possible to sell something that you are not passionate about, but when you market something you feel so passionate about, there is a marked difference in the success rate.

Be guided by your energy levels and motivation and you will know when you are on track or straying. If your energy drops and your motivation decreases, take it as a warning. Maybe what you were doing doesn't really interest or excite you as much as you first thought or maybe you are missing a couple of ingredients that would make it right. Likewise, don't do a marketing plan just for the sake of doing it. Do it because you really want to; you have a definite purpose in mind for it and you believe in it. You will get better results in the long run.

Speaking of better results, one of the best ways to ensure success is to have the right people around you. Your personal and professional support system can help pave the way to success, which brings us to the next chapter.

# Interpersonal Support Helps You Soar

*You cannot succeed by yourself. It's hard to find a rich hermit.*
—Jim Rohn

As the previous quote shows, in order to have a highly successful business, you will need to know how to work well with and effectively utilize others. In Chapter 13, we'll get into one of the best marketing strategies: strategic-referral partners. Now, let's look at who is supporting you or who is sabotaging you in your career as a coach.

## Who Is Involved with Your Coaching Business?

Do you believe that your business and all aspects of it (like the marketing side of things) are all about you? If you do, that would be a mistake. It might be your business, but it isn't all about you. It involves other people who are either directly or indirectly involved in your project. These people may be:

- Your colleagues and work associates.
- Your business partner or partners.
- Your current and past clients or customers.
- Your prospective clients.
- Your family, friends, and other personal support systems.
- Your virtual assistants and staff members.

- Your marketing consultants.
- Your web site designer.
- Your own life or business coach.
- Your graphic designer.
- Your referral sources.
- Your mentor or supervisor.
- Your marketing affiliates.
- Your neighbors who play loud music and disrupt your attention.

A lot of people are involved with the big picture. Many people contribute to or detract from the creation and success of your business at some stage or another.

## Who Is Supporting You?

Think about all the people who are involved with your business or project. These will be people who have an invested interest in your success either directly or indirectly and may be business associates or family members.

- Your spouse, for instance, may be indirectly supportive because he or she keeps the household running and takes care of the children and interruptions to insure you have uninterrupted time to focus on your work.
- You may have a colleague who is directly supportive because she offers to proofread your writing or help you set up a web site.
- You may have a boyfriend who is helpful because he insures you take time to smell the roses and may reward you by taking you out for dinner when you meet a major deadline or goal.
- Your best friend may be indirectly supportive because he offers you ideas and encouragement for everything you are accomplishing and plan to accomplish and helps keep the dream alive.

These are just examples, but I'd like you to take some time now to list all those around you who directly or indirectly are involved in your project in a helpful and useful manner:

_____

_____

_____

Can you remember their contribution? What is it they have done so far that has been helpful to you?

_____

_____

_____

If they haven't done anything just yet, what are they planning to do to contribute?

_____

_____

_____

In what ways do they demonstrate to you that you can count on them if you need to?

_____

_____

_____

It could well be that some friends plan to help you at a future stage when you are ready to actively promote your business. Each person's special talent may be offered at various stages throughout your project, and it is important you recognize and appreciate their support.

If you couldn't think of many or any supporters, could it be you are not fully utilizing the people you do know who can make a difference to your success? There is no need to struggle on alone when all you have to do is ask for help. Projects move much more smoothly when we have help, besides which, it's a lot of fun to work with other people rather than always on your own.

Mind you, everybody is different. Perhaps you are one of those who really does work better alone. Or maybe you are somebody who bounces off the walls if left to your own devices and company for too long.

Some people find their motivation from exchanging ideas and thoughts with somebody else and feel energized from this sharing. If this is you, consider doing joint ventures with colleagues or hire professional consultants and coaches who can assist you, help stimulate your creativity, and keep you focused.

Also think about including those people whom you previously have not included. You may have excluded them either because you thought their involvement was not appropriate at the time or perhaps you didn't want to impose on them. Don't write them off until you are sure they really don't have anything thing to offer support-wise. If you aren't sure, ask yourself this question: "Will I be intrusive or bothersome if I ask this person for support?"

Naturally, the only real way to find out if something will or will not work, be bothersome, and so forth is to just do it and then evaluate the result. Get out of your comfort zone and test the waters.

When you are being given help or guidance, one way to maximize your benefit from them is to let them know exactly how they are helpful. For example, if your partner supports you by offering encouragement and believing you can do it, let him know how that helps you—show appreciation and gratitude.

If you have a lack of support in your life, consider ways you can get it. Rally friends and relatives, attend professional networking groups, and generally make the effort to meet new people. You can also contact potential business partners who might add value to your project. You don't have to be all formal about it. Invite them to meet you for coffee somewhere to share ideas.

If you are more the hermit type and prefer to work on your own, take a moment to think about how having supportive people could benefit you. Write down some ways in which this support could help you be more effective and successful or even more motivated and inspired.

## Who Is Sabotaging or Enabling You?

Here is some disconcerting news: Having supportive people around you may not always be in your best interests. Some people in your life may be contributing to your self-doubt or they may be sabotaging you. Usually they are close friends or family members who believe they are protecting you from the hurtful results of failure. They lack more confidence than you do! Maybe they are timid sorts who, for one reason or another, do not have what it takes to successfully go out and do their own thing. They will openly share all their fears with you.

By this, we're not saying these people *want* you to fail, but by sharing your fears they will fuel your own self-doubts rather than help you overcome them and move ahead.

For example, maybe they have noticed that when you work on your marketing plan you become frustrated and anxious, and because they care about you and don't want to see you experiencing these emotions, they will come up with ways to help you avoid them. They will be right there with suggestions for leaving that nasty task alone and, maybe, suggest you both go clean the attic together to take your mind off it! Or maybe it is you who is considering going to clean the attic, in which case, these friends will happily go along with it rather than motivate you to stick with the task at hand.

Don't forget that avoiding your habit of avoiding is the way to overcome anxiety. The key is to face it head on and conquer it. Friends who don't allow you to do this are not serving you in a helpful manner, regardless of their well-meaning intentions. In fact, by enabling or helping you to avoid, they are actually encouraging your state of anxiety.

When you let your friends do this, you do not progress on your project. Second, your fear of the task is strengthened. Third, your avoidance is reinforced, and it is likely you will use avoidance the next time, too.

Explain this to your "helpful" friends, and tell them if they really want to be helpful, they should be encouraging about sticking with it and avoiding avoidance or procrastination. Tell them not to get involved with any frustration you feel. You don't want their sympathy, just their support to make sure you keep going. Take it one step farther, let *them* clean your attic while *you* get on with the job at hand!

You can be specific in the ways your friends can support you. Maybe you just want a cheerleader. Maybe you want them to take a firm stand with you and insist you stick with the task at hand, or else! Maybe they can support you by not popping around to visit during the hours of . . . whatever your working hours are.

We should also warn you that you may meet some people whose motives for enabling your self-sabotage are not as noble as those described previously. Unfortunately, there are people in the world who simply do not want you to be successful. This might be because they are jealous or envious of people who are more successful than themselves. It may be because they think that your victories would detract from their own achievements. Some people hate to see the new kid on the block take the limelight from them, so they'd rather see you fail.

What motivates this nastiness? Often, it is driven by their own insecurity, lack of confidence, and lack of self-worth. Don't take it personally. The best way to deal with this type of interference is to confront the offenders directly or refuse to have anything to do with them and their negative influences.

## Collaborate with Those Who Know

No one person is strong in all areas of business. We all have our strengths and weaknesses. Another benefit of positive interpersonal support is that it can help you build up your weaker areas.

Ambitious, successful, and intelligent people are characterized by their ability to surround themselves with others who can mentor and teach them. They don't hang around with losers. You can begin to search for people who have complementary skills. Look for people and qualities that you admire and aspire toward.

You can ask people if they will assist you, even if it is just to consult on your project or give you feedback. Let them know what you have to contribute and what you feel they can contribute. You can also offer to compensate them as a consultant or offer profit-sharing on your project if you can't afford to pay them outright, and you never know, maybe they'll be happy to help free of charge if not too much time and effort on their part is required.

Do consider looking for a mentor. Never be afraid to ask for guidance, assistance, or advice. One interesting point to note is if you are someone who tends to give a lot of yourself to others, you are likely to be fortunate in the responses you get from potential mentors. As with karma, what goes around, comes around. Or, you get back what you put out. Following the laws of the universe, if you choose to give out first what it is you are hoping to receive back, there is a good chance of receiving it. So if you are looking for a mentor to assist you, you might be a mentor to somebody else who can use what you have to offer them.

One word of caution on this: Don't do this if the only reason for doing so is your desire to attract your own terrific mentor! It doesn't work that way. You must give to others because you sincerely want to, regardless of whether you get anything in return. This is actually a spiritual principle. If you've read Joe Vitale's *The Attractor Factor*, it should sound familiar. You should give because helping others is meaningful and personally rewarding to you, not because you think you have to or should. Why not try this for yourself and see how it works. You may be pleasantly surprised.

Joint ventures are one of the most powerful and effective marketing strategies. Although we certainly do not want you to become mired in focusing on your weakness, it is wise to be aware of where your strengths and weaknesses lie compared with others. Then you can align yourself with others and create mutually beneficial professional relationships. For example, Larina Kase realizes that her skills do not lie in the technology arena. She has had tons of great marketing ideas, but when it comes to implementing them, she needs help. For this reason, she has several excellent people whom she hires for web services, like Angela Nielson of NicMedia.com. She also purposefully creates joint ventures with people who know technology, like Milana Leshinsky of Association of Coaching & Consulting Professionals on the web. In fact, Terri Levine and Joe Vitale also actively participate in joint ventures, too. We keep saying this and it bears repeating: If it's working for the experts, you should do it too!

If we have whetted your appetite for joint ventures, keep reading. We get into it in detail in Chapter 12. There's an interview with Milana Leshinsky in that chapter, too!

## Use Your Supports Wisely

A word about using your personal support systems: do so wisely (okay, that was three words). Be careful not to burn out your supportive people. If you have a good deal of stress with your business and need a lot of support, consider using professional support systems (therapists, coaches, consultants) rather than your personal supports.

Have you ever been around someone who's constantly venting and complaining? If so, you know how frustrating this can be and how much less you want to be around these people and help them. The last thing you want to do is burn out your friends, colleagues, and family and then not be able to rely on them.

One of the most important things for which you need your support system is to do non-work-related activities. Because building a business can be stressful, frustrating, and exhausting, you need some down time and fun time in your life. Use your supports for these things; go out for dinner, go for a long hike in the park — you know, the enjoyable things in life.

Also, do not overly rely on your support systems for referrals. This can create unnecessary tensions and can keep you from doing marketing that is truly effective. Larina remembers that when she first began her coaching business, she expected to get a bunch of referrals from friends and family. Guess how many she got. None.

At the time, Larina felt hurt that no one was helping her promote her business. Keep in mind that everyone has their own, busy life. Plus, they may help promote your services, but these people are not necessarily marketing-minded. They do not know how to sell your services.

So remember, if you want to have a lucrative coaching business, use your supports effectively and recognize when your supports aren't helping you. Surround yourself with people who help keep you motivated, rejuvenated, ambitious, and happy.

### Interview with Eva Gregory

Eva Gregory is a master coach, radio host, speaker, and author of *The Feel Good Guide to Prosperity* (San Francisco, CA: Leading Edge Publishers, 2004). Her web site, Leading Edge Coaching & Training is at http://www. LeadingEdgeCoaching.com.

**You do a lot of work on helping people attract prosperity into their lives. What are your top five recommendations to help coaches create a prosperous coaching business?**
You must have a passion for what you do to the point wild horses couldn't keep you away. For me, back in 1998, when I learned about this phenomenal profession called coaching, it was as if the light bulbs came on and the fireworks went off, and I knew this was what I'd been searching for. I've been on my honeymoon with this profession ever since!

Become extremely clear about what you want your coaching business to look like. If you had all the money in the world, all the support in the world, and could not fail, what would you dare to dream? Dare to envision? You have the entire universe on your side. What could you do with that? Be open to possibility. Dream freely and dream big!

Spend time every day basking in the joy and the wonderful feelings of that vision being fulfilled as if it were manifest *right now*. Enjoy the feelings of having your ideal coaching business *now.* Even when reality seeps in that is less than what you want, be vigilant about reaching for the visions and thoughts about your coaching business that feeeeeeeeel really good, really exciting, really yummy to you.

Get into action. And make sure they are *inspired* actions in the direction of what you want. *Inspired* means "in spirit." Coming from inspiration means coming from spirit—it feels really good! Keep a joyful focus on the vision of your ideal coaching business with every action you take.

Be unstoppable. Don't allow what you don't know to get in your way. Be willing to learn. Connect with others who've done what you aspire to any way you can. Read about them, get into their classes, buy their books and materials, hire a coach/mentor to work with you who's where you want to be.

## What are some of the limiting beliefs that keep coaches from creating prosperity?

I actually did a survey of coaches to find out what holds them back from creating prosperity in their lives. Here's what I found:

a. They don't believe in themselves or their abilities fully.
b. They believe they are put here to serve others at their own expense; that if they really want to help people, they shouldn't be charging for it—or if they do, certainly not too much.
c. They think that what comes naturally to them doesn't seem like a big deal, so why would people pay for it?
d. They believe coaching is only something someone would pay for *after* all other expenses in their lives have been handled, that coaching is expensive for most people or is seen as a luxury.
e. They believe charging money—particularly higher fees—is greedy.
f. They believe if their rates are too high, no one will pay; yet if their rates are too low, they are not valued enough.
g. It never occurred to them they could charge more. There is no abundance mentality.

*(continued)*

h. They believe if they don't have everything figured out in their own lives they don't deserve to coach others; worthiness issues.
i. They believe they have to be an expert.
j. They get stopped when they think they might not be doing it right.
k. They believe they have to be marketing wizards in order to succeed, that it is hard to attract clients, they are few and far between.
l. They are afraid to market themselves; they are afraid of rejection.
m. They feel like failures when their clients don't achieve success; they feel responsible for their client's lack of success; they get attached to their client's results. In other words, they believe any failure on their client's part is a failure for themselves.
n. They mistakenly attach the *time* they spend on the phone with clients to the rate they charge rather than the *value* they provide their clients.
o. They believe you can only make the big bucks in the corporate world.
p. They don't believe success can ever happen to them because it hasn't been their experience up to this point.
q. They believe they can help others succeed but cannot succeed themselves.
r. They don't know how to deal with success.
s. They aren't committed; they treat it as a hobby or a nice idea; they don't take coaching seriously as a business.
t. They are poor business owners.

**How can utilizing your support systems (both personal and professional) help attract prosperity?**
Over the years, I developed a comprehensive program in which I work with folks to help them establish and achieve their desired objectives.

Individuals begin identifying limiting beliefs and behaviors, breaking through old thought patterns, moving through residual barriers that no longer serve them as they hone and tweak their ideal vision and take inspired actions in every area of their lives. Building a strong foundation for personal prosperity and fulfillment in this system includes coaching, telephone discussions, brainstorming sessions, support, mastermind groups, and activities to keep their momentum going toward the goals and achievements they've identified.

This support system and the processes within it work regardless of how much education you may have, how much money, intelligence, or experience you have. The great news is none of those things matter! What does matter is where you put your focus, on moving toward what you *do* want and identifying the *inspired actions* that will get you there—as I like to say (thanks Catherine Ponder!), "in an easy and relaxed manner, in a healthy and positive way."

That means holding the focus on *you*, your desires, and your goals as well as developing, increasing, and enhancing your income streams. This system is designed to shift your thinking onto a higher level of vibration, where bigger visions reside and big ideas abound.

Because it takes time for new habits—of behavior or thought—to get locked into our consciousness, I wanted to create a system that would last long enough for those new habits to become an integral part of the individuals who participate so that the lives they desire to lead are their new habit rather than the exception to the rule. It is the day-in, day-out continuity that makes the difference in whether someone absorbs new ways of being, living, and thinking for the long-term or not. Results can be so much greater when over a longer period of time individuals can be consciously guided and simple changes made before getting too far off the mark of their desired outcomes.

What I have learned is that under the proper coaching program, the learning process is much deeper and more permanent. There is no limit to what's possible.

Letting go of old patterns of thought and old behaviors as you hold your vision and your focus in the direction of your goals and aspirations, living within a much more effective paradigm and a strong support system, you begin to feel more freedom, and life feels more rewarding.

*(continued)*

**How do you think beliefs, support, and prosperity are related?**

I don't believe relying on others is what creates or doesn't create prosperity or success in one's life. It all comes down to your belief systems within yourself, and based on the beliefs you hold, you can attract into your life success and prosperity—which obviously includes others in your life and your experience that may be the stepping stones to that success, instrumental in your success—such as mentors, coaches, experts, friends, or family members that believe in you and so forth. By the same token, based on your belief systems, you can attract others and means that do not create success in your life. In either case, however, it isn't about relying on anything more than the beliefs you hold.

**Whose support has been instrumental in achieving the success as a coach that you have, and how has it helped you?**

Two very important mentors are Bob Proctor and Jim Rohn. Another important and profound influence in my life has been the teachings of Abraham through Jerry and Esther Hicks, where I was first introduced to universal laws many years ago.

These masters have shared massive amounts of wisdom and knowledge with me. In fact, the most transformational point for me was when I began applying these teachings to my own life. I learned exactly how universal laws work and now understand exactly how to align my thoughts, feelings, and actions in harmony with what I want as well as integrating tangible, practical steps within this framework—an important step!

In fact, Terri Levine was my personal coach for a while and has been highly instrumental in showing me how to integrate the practical steps with being a successful entrepreneur, CEO, and business owner to the teachings I learned about universal laws into my life and my business.

The impact my mentors' work, ideas, processes, and systems have left with me is a powerful new awareness and perspective on life. As this transformation took place, it was clear to me I could never return to my old way of thinking, much less my old way of being—nor would I want to!

And now, my work (play!) is sharing it with others ready to experience the same.

# 9

# Beat Avoidance and Procrastination

*You miss one hundred percent of the shots you don't take.*
—Wayne Gretzky

If you are already working as a coach, you have certainly experienced times when you have avoided doing something that would help you grow your business or become a better coach. You might have put off making some important cold calls. Or maybe you delayed hiring a mentor coach or a business coach of your own, telling yourself that you couldn't afford it. Perhaps you decided to wait until next month to attend a great networking dinner. Sound familiar?

If you are just getting started with your coaching career, you may have already experienced some procrastination about getting started or getting training. You may be taking a long time to read books or may have already delayed some educational opportunities. Let's nip these behaviors in the bud because they are sure to hold you back.

Avoidance is almost always associated with some level of fear or anxiety. Here's how.

## How Anxiety and Avoidance Develop and Grow

Avoidance and procrastination are behaviors that are fueled by anxiety and self-doubt. People very often choose *not* to try something because they feel it is better *not* to do it than do it and fail miserably! Nobody wants to fail.

For example, authors know only too well that awful feeling when they sit down to write and get writer's block. Nothing comes to them! They can't write a thing! So what do they do? They will do anything to escape that awful feeling. They will distract themselves by checking their e-mail or cleaning out their desk — even if they hate cleaning (or, as Terri Levine says, they'll even clean the attic!).

Then what happens? When they go back and sit down to write again, they automatically experience anxiety because they have been adversely conditioned that when they sit to write, their minds go blank.

When a specific activity (working on a book or building a coaching or consulting business) has been coupled with a negative reaction (anxiety, frustration, annoyance), people are more likely to experience the negative reaction the next time they engage in that specific activity.

In psychology, this is the process of conditioning — aversive conditioning.

This is how that works. Imagine you developed a stomach virus, so you aren't feeling the greatest to begin with. So, when you sit down to eat a certain food, you become sick. (The food didn't make you sick, the virus did.) Your brain doesn't know that, however, and the next time you smell or taste that very same food, it is highly likely that you will have a negative reaction of some kind. The same process can happen with working on your coach training and development and business building.

And there is another type of conditioning: escape conditioning. To make the aversive response (anxiety, irritation) stop, people choose to escape from the situation. They run away from it. If we use the analogy of the author and his writer's block, of course, initially he will feel better when he turns off his computer and turns on his favorite TV show. The problem with doing this, however, is that we escape from the negative feelings before we have the chance to get through them and potentially develop positive feelings in the situation. Running away truly doesn't solve anything! When the author avoids writing when the blank screen causes discomfort, she learns that the way to get rid of the uncomfortable feeling is to escape, making it more likely that she'll avoid it the next time.

## The Procrastination Solution

Initially, you may not like the solution, but when you try it and discover it works, you will probably change your mind, so don't dismiss this until you try it. The solution is to always confront the things that make you anxious and stay in the situation long enough that your negative reaction subsides. Trust us, this works. We've all used this technique and found it very effective. And it gets easier with practice.

This process reduces avoidance, and it is actually the same process that works with any type of anxiety. Have you heard of the anxiety disorder called obsessive-compulsive disorder (OCD)? One well-known example of OCD is the sufferer who feels they must always wash their hands. This sufferer may obsess about getting sick if they do not keep everything spotlessly clean and, therefore, hygienic. They avoid any potential contact with contaminants like dirt, and the moment they feel they might have, they have an immediate compulsion to go wash their hands. By avoiding any contact with potential contaminants, they are merely reinforcing or increasing their obsessive-compulsive disorder.

For them, the cure is to allow themselves to come into contact with potential contaminants and not give in to their compulsion to go wash themselves until their anxiety levels come down. Anxiety levels *do go down*. When you first start practicing this method, don't expect instant results, but continue with it and you'll discover that your anxiety level will go down. This works for OCD and all other forms of anxiety and avoidance. It may not be easy when you first try it, but it will become easier.

Next time you experience negative feelings about working on your business or your training or marketing, you need to push through those feelings and get yourself to do it anyway. Don't give in to your "compulsion" to go clean the attic until your anxious or negative feelings have passed, and by then, you probably won't feel like cleaning the attic anyway! In fact, after your initial reaction, you will get going and will have a positive experience. This will also make it much easier and more enjoyable the next time.

In addition, your confidence will start to increase as you begin getting results that you feel good about, and your avoidance and procrastination will start to decrease.

The key to success with this approach is that you *keep doing the activity that you wanted to avoid until a positive result occurs.*

What sort of positive result? It could be something like coming up with a great new idea or coming up with the initial stages of a great marketing plan. It could even be something as simple as noticing your level of frustration or your negative feelings starting to decrease.

When you first decide to stop avoiding or procrastinating, it may feel like it's taking a while; humans like instant results and instant gratification. The human body naturally habituates to anxiety within sometime between a few minutes and around 90 minutes. After the initial adrenaline rush (from the sympathetic nervous system being activated), the parasympathetic nervous system kicks in and produces a more relaxed feeling.

The key to remember is to stick with what you're doing for a while so you do not create an escape conditioning response, because if you do give in and escape, it will happen again next time, and the feeling may be even stronger. If you keep sticking with your difficult situation on repeated occasions, you will find that the time for a positive result to occur begins to get quicker and quicker.

If you remember nothing else from this section, remember this: *Avoid avoiding.*

Avoidance makes the situation feel worse. Avoidance makes it more difficult to accomplish your goals over time. The more you avoid, the worse it gets.

Nike got it right with their motto: *Just do it.*

## The Paradox of Perfectionism

Believe it or not, perfectionism is actually considered to be a form of anxiety.

Think about this. When you feel like something *has to be perfect,* how do you feel? Calm, tranquil, and relaxed? No. The need to make something perfect puts you under a lot of pressure.

Seeking perfection makes it difficult for you to begin something and finish it. It interferes with efficiency and time-management skills. It makes you focus on extraneous, unimportant details. Perfectionism destroys confidence because you will *never* feel good enough. You will never be satisfied even with terrific results because they're not perfect, in your eyes!

Perfectionism interferes with:

- Beginning a marketing plan because you can't come up with the perfect copy, title, or target audience.
- Writing your plan because you may feel that all conditions need to be perfect for you to effectively work on it. You may think that you need to be in the mood to do it, have a large block of time, and have the right working conditions. All of the stars in the universe would need to be aligned to create these conditions. It can take centuries for this to happen. Do you have centuries?
- Finishing your plan because you think that it cannot be done until it is perfect. You may worry about how you will judge yourself or how others will judge you negatively if it is not perfect.

Perfectionism can be rewarding and reinforcing because when you have this belief, you may actually get things done perfectly. This is also why it can be difficult to give up perfectionism.

*But* think about what you could get done if you gave up perfectionism. Ask yourself where it is really getting you and how it may be holding you back or contributing to self-sabotage. Is it better to write one perfect article that 50 people read or five great (but not perfect) articles that 500 people read? You decide.

Does it make you feel anxious about doing things just right? Does it make you work more slowly and go over (and over and over) your work? Does it annoy other people because you want to hold them to your rigid standards? Being perfect is not all that it is cracked up to be!

With perfectionistic thoughts and behaviors you may finish one project and make it 100 percent excellent. Without perfectionistic thoughts and behaviors, you may accomplish *six projects* that are all 97 percent excellent. Guess what, most people do not notice the 3 percent difference between the 97 percent and the 100 percent. You do the math. It's really not worth getting gray hairs over!

In order to get over perfectionism, you will need to do something radical. You've probably guessed what that radical thing will be: You will simply need to do things *not* perfectly for a while!

In fact, by your standards, you will need to mess up a couple of things.

Sound completely crazy? It is, but you need to learn that you can mess up something a bit and not suffer any major negative consequences. In fact, you'll probably still receive praise because it's quite probable that your idea of awful is everybody else's highly acceptable.

You can complete something only 85 percent perfectly and the world will not come crashing down. Teach yourself the lesson that you can be an extremely valuable, intelligent, interesting person and an excellent coach or consultant without being perfect. Being imperfect is not fatal—it's the accepted way of being on this planet. Only perfectionists expect perfection, and thank goodness they are outnumbered, or we'd all be in trouble!

## Time-Management Problems

Another problem that can lead to procrastination involves time management. Many people have difficulty with scheduling their time and sticking to a schedule. We don't like the stricture of feeling like we need to stick to a schedule; it can take some of the fun and spontaneity out of our daily lives. We fear that we will miss out on other opportunities if we stick with a schedule or that we will not have the flexibility to handle things as they arise. Admittedly, it can be a juggling act.

### *Create a Structure, Even If You Don't Want One*

It can seem strange to schedule things with yourself. It is like making an appointment to meet with yourself, but it's very useful if it helps you keep on track and keep up with everything.

As much as we may rebel against and resist making a structure for ourselves, it is very important. After working with top executives and performers and community leaders, it has become clear that the people who manage their time well are the people who structure it and schedule it. Makes sense when you think about it.

If you have an assistant, then your time may already be scheduled for you. Your assistant may not know that you need to schedule time for marketing work. Be sure to let them know how much time and when to put it into your schedule.

If you create your own schedule, get in the habit of making your schedule for the week or month and then updating it each evening or morning. Use technology to help you. Synchronize a pocket PC with your desktop or laptop computer. Create reminders that pop up and tell you what you are supposed to be working on. There is new software that may help you here. See Joe Vitale's Intention Creator at http://www.IntentionCreator.com. If you use Microsoft Outlook as your e-mail program, you can also use the Outlook calendar and task features, both of which provide pop-up reminders that appear on your screen and come with so-called snooze buttons so you can defer the reminder and have it repeated at any intervals from five minutes up to one week.

If you cannot afford or do not have or do not like using technology to help you, a good old-fashioned pad of paper or calendar will work just fine. Create one page that has a running list of tasks that need to be completed and then add the tasks into specific time slots in your day.

For example, many people feel that they need to wait for inspiration to strike before they can really produce something of quality. They feel they need to be in the mood. Well, you could be waiting a long time. We all go through these dry patches occasionally—we may be overworked, tired, ill—but if something is worth doing, it is worth doing, right? Instead of deferring something, waiting for that perfect moment when all the stars are lined up and you are feeling superinspired, plan to write or market and allow inspiration to unfold as you get into it. This very often happens and is a trick used by authors. They just keep writing, and eventually their writer's block disappears.

Form follows function, as they say in the art world. The function is your time scheduled to work on your marketing plan and starting to get some ideas down on a page. The form is the inspiration and thoughts that begin to flow after you get started.

A good red flag is any thought that begins with, "I'm just going to wait for. . . ."

Don't wait for anything. Put it into your schedule and then stick to your schedule.

### Goal-Setting Will Improve Your Use of Time

Funnily enough, many people do not like to create goals. They feel that making goals can put artificial limits on things and take valuable time to think of and write down. They also doubt the effectiveness of this exercise.

"I can't be bothered writing down my goals," a bright entrepreneur once said. "I like to live my life spontaneously and take things as they come. I like to go with my intuition and follow my gut."

He obviously understands his natural inclinations and strengths. He is a highly intuitive person. A born entrepreneur with a nose for the next big thing. He actually began several successful companies.

So, what's the problem, then, you ask?

The problem is he did not set any goals, and his businesses did not achieve anywhere near the goals that they were capable of meeting. And not having written goals meant he was also unaware of how his businesses were doing; he had nothing by which to gauge their success.

Often our greatest strengths also serve as our greatest weaknesses.

His spontaneity, free spirit, and zest for entrepreneurship served him well. His inability to plan, manage time, and accomplish important tasks served him poorly.

In the process of coaching and learning how to set and achieve goals, he learned how to manage his time and stay focused on the *important* tasks. He became able to rely on his intuition but then also use it to get things done.

Although some of his initial concerns about the limits that goals can place on you can certainly be true at times, and there is a lot of individual difference in terms of what types of goals work best, there is a great deal of evidence that shows we tend to accomplish that which is:

1. Written down.
2. Put into our schedule at a specific point in time.
3. In very specific terms.
4. Has some degree of flexibility built in.

When you do not have specifically laid out goals, you are less likely to actually work on meeting your goals. You are also less likely to accomplish that goal because you will not have a clear idea of what it is.

Trying to work toward an undefined goal is like driving at night with no lights on your car. You will not see where you are going.

If you don't know where you're going, any road will take you there.

— *"Any Road" by George Harrison*

You need to know your target and have an idea of how you are going to get there. Without this information, you will waste a great deal of time heading out of your way or trying to figure out where you are going. You can get lost. You can waste precious time. You can make silly mistakes.

Goal-setting theory tells us that it is not only important to set goals but how you set goals is also critical. A goal of "work on marketing plan and finish it by the end of the month" is unlikely to cut it.

You may have heard of creating *SMART goals* to motivate you. (If not, pay extra attention, this is a great thing to use with your coaching clients, too.) This concept was created by an unknown marketing and motivational genius. Creating and sticking to SMART goals can change your life, especially if you have not been using goal-setting in this way.

A SMART goal is one that is:

Specific.
Measurable.
Action-focused.
Realistic.
Time-limited.

Good goals can greatly help you better structure and use your time because they have a time component built right in. For a goal to be SMART, you must know what exactly it is that you want to do and how you will know when it is done (specific and measurable). You must make it a behavioral or action-focused goal. The goal must be something that you can actually do, and you should have a specific deadline in place.

For example, some good SMART goals are:

1. *Conduct a market survey of my target market (by sending out an e-mail survey to my list) to gather data, and analyze the data by April 21.*
2. *Spend three hours today researching resources for my advertisement that will introduce my service and tell readers how I will be helpful to them.*
3. *In four hours today, finish the last two sections of my marketing plan, write a sales letter, and go over these two things with my marketing consultant.*

Goals can change. You may come up with a better idea along the way to reaching a goal, and you can, and should, adjust your goal accordingly. It is best not to be a perfectionist about your goals, either. They are a plan for us to follow so we get to where we want to be. Life does throw us curve balls occasionally, and if one is aimed at you and you miss your goal by a number of days or even weeks or months, it doesn't matter as long as you persevere and keep going.

## Let's Move On

Now that you are aware and equipped with strategies to overcome all the things that may hold you back from becoming a very successful coach, you are ready to move on and get more clients.

As you read through the second half of the book, which focuses on building and marketing your coaching business, spot the excuses that come up about why you think you can't do the things we describe. Be aware whether any specific fearful or negative thoughts come to mind. Recognize problems with getting started or studying and how your focus strays from your goals. Think about how you can use supports to best help you implement your marketing strategies or take a break from marketing. And, most importantly, don't procrastinate. Start putting these ideas to work today so you can start seeing results now!

# PART 2

# Marketing Secrets of Top Coaches in Action

# 10

# Setting Up Your Coaching Business

*Good business leaders create a vision, articulate the vision, passionately own the vision, and relentlessly drive it to completion.*

—Jack Welch

## "I Don't Know How to Build a Business"

To be an excellent coach, you do not need to hold a master's degree in business management. You may be the most effective coach in the world, however, but if you aren't able to set up and market your business, you won't be able to help that many people. The last thing you want to be is the world's best-kept secret.

According to research by Stephen Fairley, author of *Getting Started in Personal and Executive Coaching,* the average coach makes less than $10,000 in their first year. This income wouldn't exactly motivate and excite you, would it? Respondents to his survey also indicated 53 percent of coaches earn less than $20,000 per year, and only 9 percent of coaches earn more than $100,000 per year. These numbers tell us that many coaches do not know how to build a coaching business.

There are basic steps to take as a coaching-business owner. First, there are decisions about how you set up your business. Then you need to figure out how to create business and then how to operate the business. We'll touch on each one.

# Organization of the Business

The first step is to determine how to set up your business. You must decide if your business will be a sole proprietorship, partnership, corporation, or limited liability company (LLC).

### Sole Proprietorships

Our recommendation for a new business owner is to begin as a sole proprietor because this is a simple format. The primary advantage to a sole proprietorship is its simplicity. Your accountant's fees will be lower, and you won't need to pay to set up a corporation or LLC. Sole proprietorships consist of you as sole business owner and operator. This is a common business entity for many coaching businesses. It is not a corporation, so it does not have the same level of protection of assets that you would find with a corporation. With a sole proprietorship, all assets are exposed (meaning up for grabs in a lawsuit) if you are unmarried. If you have a spouse, you can hold assets under your joint names or in your spouse's name for some level of asset protection.

### Corporations and LLCs

As your business expands and you have significant revenues, it may then be time to incorporate for liability protection. Wait until you have several clients, and then you can sit down with your accountant to get guidance on the best way for you to protect your company.

Some of the benefits of incorporating your business include:

- Tax benefits (which vary, based on what type of business entity you create).
- Clear distributions of profits or dividends.
- Reduced personal liability and exposure of personal assets.
- Enhanced corporate image for marketing purposes.
- Enhanced corporate image for loan procurement.

There are many types of corporations, which are best explained by an attorney. Larina Kase interviewed Henry C. Fader, Esq., a corporate and healthcare partner at Pepper Hamilton LLP, Attorneys at Law, a national firm based in Philadelphia (faderh@pepperlaw.com), for the book *The Successful Therapist* to get some detailed information. He described the following types of corporate entities:

An *S-Corp* is a business corporation that requires an election by the owner and shareholders. This type of corporation avoids taxation at the corporate level. All the money taxed is considered to be profit.

A *C-Corp* is a business corporation that is subject to taxation at both the business and shareholder levels. If you were the employee, you would receive a salary. The corporation pays taxes on the profits for the year. If you're paying dividends to the owner (yourself), you are then paying taxes again. The advantage is that you can choose your fiscal year, and it can be something other than a calendar year. Many professionals do this to shift income from one year to the next, depending on which months are the busiest, so they can stay within certain tax brackets. For instance, if your coaching business is slow over the summer, you can shift your calendar year to use the slow period to your advantage.

A *limited liability corporation (LLC)* has the tax-status attributes of an S-Corp: no taxation at the LLC level. The reason people like to use it is its flexibility in determining who gets profits and when. In your operating agreement, you can determine how profits are distributed (e.g., 90/10 owners can distribute profits 50/50). Some things are deductible for tax purposes in an LLC that are not deductible with other corporate structures. For instance, with an S-Corp, you can't typically deduct health insurance, whereas with an LLC you can.

### Partnerships

If you find later that you prefer not to work alone, you might want to add a business partner. Many coaches do this because it creates a nice image of stability and a natural support system.

### The Benefits of a Partnership

As you know, two (or more) minds are often better than one. Having a business partner can help you develop a more creative, innovative company. When we come up with ideas on our own, we have less incentive and structure to challenge ourselves than when we are accountable to our business partner. A partnership can also result in better products because it often serves as a checks-and-balances system. Our partner can push us to work harder to catch errors and can identify and rectify the errors when they do occur. All three of us have partnered in some way with others and produced programs or products. In fact, we've done so for this very book!

A business partnership can also serve as a method to decrease your anxiety about running your own company. You know that between the two of you, problems will get solved because you will work together until you solve them. It is good to know that you have someone else who is equally invested in getting situations resolved optimally. When your partner has skills that you do not have, you do not have to worry about those areas as much.

Another great thing is that you always have someone to chat with. This can help ease the loneliness of running your own home-based business. After working with many solo entrepreneurs, we have often heard, "No one really understands what I am going through with my business." This is often true when you are building a business on your own. When you have a business partner, however, you have someone to help you cope with the stress, who can truly empathize with the difficulties, and who is constantly there to talk about the business.

### *The Problems with Partnerships*

A business partnership is essentially like a marriage. You need to look at it as a partnership for the long term. You do not want to rush into it without first feeling as though you know one another well enough to determine whether you can work together day in and day out.

Many partners select one another for their complementary business skills, which is a great idea except that partnerships work much better when personalities are not constantly clashing. After the honeymoon period wears off, you could realize that you do not get along or do not really like each other. Some personality incompatibilities can help balance out a partnership and enhance the business's performance. For instance, if you are laid back and a bit of a procrastinator, whereas your partner is a go-getter and very organized, you can balance each other out quite well.

Disagreements may also arise regarding how to run the business. These disagreements may stem from personality differences. For instance, if someone is very conservative and cautious, whereas the partner is a risk taker, conflicts can arise regarding hiring, expansion, or investment decisions. Working with a consultant or coach before beginning your business can be an excellent idea to work through all of these issues. As coaches, we work with business partners before they officially create their partnership agreements to help them gain clarity and understanding of one another's positions. We have been putting their ideas and agreements in writing so they can refer to them later as disagreements arise.

One of the other problems with creating a partnership is that if you decide to end the business or if one partner decides to leave, it can be more complicated than if you were in business by yourself. Of course, you would include provisions for company dissolution or partner buyout in your partnership agreement, so these factors would be accounted for ahead of time.

One option is to create a limited partnership. A *limited partnership* is a partnership in which at least two people are business partners. One is the general partner, and one is the limited partner. The limited partner gets limited liability, which means that a creditor cannot sue the limited partner for more than their investment (like a corporation), but the general partner can be sued for more. These structures are not very common in professional situations.

## Marketing and Building Your Business

You can be the greatest coach in the world, but if you don't market your business, your business will exist as a secret, and you won't have many clients or any clients. You must create a list of marketing strategies that you will enact to have people find out about your business and services.

Some marketing strategies to include are:

Advertising.
Direct mail.
Web site.
E-mail marketing.
Newsletter.
Public speaking.
Public relations.
Networking.

You want to take a look at each of these areas and come up with marketing actions for each one. Then put the actions on a yearly calendar and perform each one. We will get into detail on some of these strategies in later chapters.

Every business on the planet needs to market itself. Even the Avon ladies knocking on doors and leaving their brochures are doing marketing.

If you think that because you lack the experience or background to market your business you'll be doomed to failure, then you're wrong. We know too many coaches who not only didn't have the first idea about how to market their business but were terrified of the prospect as well who have gone on to find enjoyable marketing methods that worked great.

Let's just say you pass your coaching examination with flying colors. You're one of the smartest coaches in your area. If you do not advertise and market your business, nobody will know about you. If nobody knows about you, how are you going to get clients? How are you going to be in business?

Fear of marketing can also sabotage completing your studies or the exam. Because you know that's the next step for you and you don't feel ready for it. In fact, you may be dreading it! If you don't finish your studies or do the exam, then, of course, you won't have to worry about marketing, will you?

There are a lot of myths about marketing, and most people's fears are unfounded. They have stereotypical ideas in their head that turn them off the very idea. Most people believe they are not good at marketing or selling. They may even have the used car salesman who sold them a lemon as their idea of a marketer or sales person. And who trusts them, right? Marketers have to blow their own horn. Who believes people who blow their own horn?

It's only natural to have doubts or experience a lack of confidence in any area in which you have no experience. You haven't tried, so how do you know? It's your negative self-talk again. Your fears. Some people are so afraid of marketing that it completely stops them from considering any kind of business opportunity. No matter how miserable they are, they'd rather stay in their dead-end, boring, poorly paid job than have to go out and market a business of their own.

The closer you get to the end of your study or exam completion, the more likely this fear will raise its head. The fear that what if your marketing efforts are pitiful and fail could mean all the money and time you've spent so far were wasted. You'll look like a fool as well as a failure. Do you wonder why your motivation levels drop when you start worrying about marketing?

Many new coaches fear marketing. "I'm a coach, not a marketer! What do I know about marketing?" Terri Levine is so used to hearing these fears that she has developed special programs and courses specifically for coaches to market their businesses. Techniques that work. Techniques that are easy. She uses them and has seen them work—for her business and for others'—so now when she hears somebody say they can't or won't be able to market, she just laughs because she knows the truth—as we all do—and we hope you will, too, very soon!

The problem with a lack of self-confidence in ourselves and our abilities is that the fears we conjure get in the way of rational thinking. How many times have you met somebody, adult or child, who was convinced they couldn't do it (whatever "it" happened to be at the time), and then with a little encouragement and a bit of help, they went ahead and did it as if they'd always been doing it?

How do you know what you can or cannot do until you have tried? When some people are faced with something new and unknown, it's only natural for them to wonder if they can do it. That's okay. It's when they say definitely that they can't do it that it becomes a problem. It's one of the ways in which people sabotage themselves.

Maybe it is not the marketing in itself that freezes you and keeps you from moving forward. Maybe it is your belief about what marketing is and how it is done that is holding you back. Maybe you think you have to spend thousands of dollars to make your marketing effective. Maybe you don't have these thousands of dollars available to spend on marketing. If you believe you need a lot of money to make your marketing effective, you will soon find other things to do that you can afford to do now, such as cleaning the attic and put off marketing your business for another time.

If you have convinced yourself that you're no salesperson and you hate marketing (even if you're never personally tried it), you will lack the motivation to give it your best try. As with any endeavor, successful marketing requires not only careful planning but also a determination to succeed. You may have to try several techniques before you find the one that really works for you and your business and that you don't mind doing.

The best way to bump this fear on the head is to educate yourself. You will be pleasantly surprised to find there is more than one way to market a business, and many ways are quite inexpensive (read more about this in Chapter 15). Learn what you can about the various marketing methods. We fear the unknown. Make marketing known to you and you will lose the fear. (Check the Recommended Resources at the back of the book, where you will find marketing courses and kits to help you discover how easy marketing can be.)

You must not give up if your first marketing attempt is not successful. In marketing, you must be patient and persistent and not give up a method without giving it a fair trial. Many marketing techniques will not provide instant results; results come about with repetition, persistence, and patience. Marketing research shows that it takes an average of five to seven exposures to something before the consumer is ready to buy. If you're expecting instant miracles, you may be setting yourself up for a letdown, which in turn will knock your self-confidence levels and motivation and bring back those self-defeating behaviors and self-talk.

Maybe you believe that only specialist marketers can market successfully and that because you cannot afford to hire one of these marketing experts, you'll never be able to market your business. It's a good thing that this isn't true, otherwise we'd all be in trouble! Take Joe Vitale, for example. If he had thought that he couldn't get into Internet marketing because he wasn't an expert, he never would have become one, would he? Check out his chapter on Internet marketing and learn that anyone can be an expert marketer if they try.

Don't compare yourself to any marketer and think that because they have more experience than you do in their specialized niche that obviously they'd succeed where you'd fail. You can learn what they know very quickly, and then the only difference will be that they choose to work in that area as their profession, whereas you choose to work in coaching.

## Financing Your Business

Lack of capitalization is one of the primary causes of small-business failures within the first two years, so the financing of your coaching business is extremely important.

The financing for your coaching business can come from savings or loans. If you're using mostly savings, you want to have enough capital saved to cover several months of your operating expenses plus all of your start-up costs. Luckily, many of the start-up expenses (like your web site and computer) are costs that are not reoccurring. The reoccurring costs for coaching businesses are not very high, but they do add up, so think of everything from web site hosting to e-mail newsletter mailing to your telephone plan when creating your budget.

The United States Small Business Administration (SBA) offers SBA loans that may be applicable to your practice or company idea. Their general web site can be found at http://www.sba.gov/. It is also an extremely good source of information for many aspects of starting a business.

To apply for a loan, look at the page http://www.sba.gov/financing/basics/applyloan.html. You will need a business plan and a financial plan, including your balance sheets. A nice example of a completed balance sheet is provided at http://www.toolkit.cch.com/tools/downloads/balsheet.xlt.

Another source of funding is through investors. Keep in mind that selling ownership in the business reduces your level of control over your company. One type of investor is a silent partner who owns a portion of the business but does not want any level of control over the operations of the company. Another type of investor is the venture capitalist. These are firms that range in size from individual venture capitalists to very large corporations of investors. Venture capitalists seek out investment opportunities that offer a very high potential growth rate, so the majority of coaching businesses would typically not be attractive to venture capitalists. Some companies that can potentially expand nationally or internationally would be, however. Venture capitalists want to see companies that have serious potential and can eventually become publicly traded on the stock market. Individual venture capitalists are sometimes referred to as *angel investors*.

It is estimated that approximately 80 percent of small businesses fail in their first five years. We tell you this not to scare you but to make you approach your coaching business seriously. If you look at it as a hobby that you will do to earn some extra income, you will be at risk. Instead, if you decide to begin a coaching company, you want to do so with the mindset and behaviors that predict success and not failure.

## Get Moving Now!

There you have it. Coaching is the number one home-based business in the United States and the fastest growing home-based business. All that is missing is *you!*

What actions are you committed to taking *now* to start and succeed as a coach?

Look through this chapter several times and make a list of the actions you need to take, then don't wait. Take some action now and begin to create or build your coaching business. In the coming chapters, we'll reveal the marketing secrets of the pros to help your coaching business take off!

# 11

# Making Marketing Fun

*People rarely succeed unless they have fun in what they are doing.*
— Dale Carnegie

## How Can Something Stressful Be Fun?

For many coaches, marketing is stressful. You worry. "Should I spend money on this marketing strategy?" "Will I be able to earn enough income to pay the bills?" "Will I look like a fool when I get up to talk?" "Will I be able to do marketing right, and if I do, will I be able to sell?" There are tons of concerns that can arise when you think of marketing your practice.

It may be a bit stressful for you, or it may be the worst part of your coaching career. Because coaching is a business, it will be very tough for you to be successful without marketing—and that applies to *any* business. Now that you've worked on all the things that may hold you back from becoming a successful coach, let's jump into marketing and all the enjoyment and rewards that it can bring you.

Of course, once you are successful, your marketing will start taking care of itself. But you'll always have to market. There's no way around this. Either you or someone you hire will have to market for you. As soon as you stop, the well of business will begin to dry.

One of the ironies about marketing and sales is that when you want it to be easy (at the beginning), it's not. When you don't need the business, it's easy (well, sometimes). This is similar to how celebrities get offered all kinds of free clothes and goodies when they're the ones who can actually afford a $2,000 handbag!

Once you're well known, people will approach you for interviews. You'll have a large, receptive mailing list to which you can market. Your products will be out there earning income for you and marketing your business. You'll have a team of associates lining up to do joint ventures with you. Your name will be out there. Doesn't this sound great? Now you can see how fun marketing is! It may not start out fun, but it certainly becomes exciting as it brings business. To get to this point, you'll need to master marketing and sales. *C'mon! Stop hiding. We know you're there!*

## The Fun Ones First

If you have a hard time getting going with your marketing, then start with what's exciting for you. You can tell which strategies are motivating by noticing your energy. Recall from the chapter on motivation that the best way to track motivation is by looking at your energy.

Joe Vitale says marketing is actually just sharing. If you truly believe in what you are doing, then not telling people about it is a crime. If you can help them, why aren't you telling the world? Joe says that you don't want to share, you want to sell. Share your passion, your love, your stories. Let people catch your fire.

Some marketing strategies really are enjoyable. Imagine that you arrange a lunch with a potential referral partner. Over a delicious meal, you discuss your careers and how you can help each other. By the end of the meal, you are both so enthusiastic about each other's work that you already have several clients in mind to refer to each other. You follow up the next day, and voilà! You have three excellent prospects! Now this is fun!

Imagine that you spend an hour writing an article on a topic that is very meaningful to you. It ends up being published, and you get dozens of e-mails about it and about your services. A reporter hears about your article and calls you for an interview. An article about you is written in your local newspaper, giving your business a lot of free publicity.

When marketing works, it is definitely rewarding on many levels. To get going, begin with what feels the least intimidating and most enjoyable. Once you have the momentum going, you can embark on the strategies that are more daunting, frustrating, boring, or challenging.

# Active or Passive?

One way to figure out which strategies work well for you is to see which ones better match your personality. Typically, people who are more extroverted tend to feel more motivated by active (or, more specifically, interactive) strategies. Extroverts, by definition, are those who get their energy or relaxation from being around other people. Introverts are those who prefer to do solitary activities for enjoyment or to unwind. People who are more introverted or reserved often gravitate to the passive strategies.

Keep in mind, the most effective marketing plans typically use a marketing mix of passive and active strategies. If you are introverted and dislike many of the active strategies, begin with the passive strategies and then find ways to make active strategies more palatable.

Many people dislike the classification of active versus passive because really no marketing tactics are passive. The label *passive* implies that they don't involve any work, which certainly isn't true. Here we will discuss active strategies as things that get you out and about, interacting with others, and passive strategies will be presented as the things you do on your own, often in front of your computer, understanding that they certainly involve work.

## *Active Marketing Strategies*

Here we look at some of the most powerful marketing strategies for building your coaching business. We'll think of how to take the stress out of them and make them more fun.

## *Public Speaking*

Do you enjoy getting up and speaking in front of people? Or does this idea make you tremble just thinking about it?

If you answered "yes!" to the first question, then get out and start booking some workshops right away. Any form of public speaking, whether it's seminars, keynote addresses, or workshops, is excellent marketing. With service businesses like coaching, prospects need to feel like they know, trust, and like you. What better way is there to accomplish this objective than meeting dozens or hundreds of people at once by public speaking?

If you answered "yes!" to the second question, then you may not want to begin your marketing plan with conducting workshops. *But* do not rule out public speaking altogether because it is one of the very best marketing tactics for coaching businesses. Think about which aspects of speaking in public make you uncomfortable, and begin with talks that minimize those feared aspects. For example, if you are more nervous in front of large groups of people, plan to do a small workshop in the office of a chiropractor with a staff of three. Of course, you can also do programs like Toastmasters to help gain comfort with public speaking.

Another excellent way to gently ease your shy ways into public speaking is to talk on radio. Nobody can see you there! It's just you and the radio announcer, and sometimes, you can even conduct your talk or interview over the phone from the comfort of your own home. Nothing is impossible!

Here are some locations to start looking at for giving talks. Ask yourself where your target clients are or where your potential referral partners are and speak there:

- Offices of other professionals ( physicians, lawyers, etc.).
- Universities, for faculty or students or for continuing education for alumni.
- Professional conferences and meetings.
- Organizations like Lions Club, Kiwanis, Chambers of Commerce.
- Networking group meetings and dinners.
- Nonprofit organizations.
- Businesses where your target clients work or are customers.

*Networking*

If you love going out and meeting new people, then of course, networking is fun. If you feel uncomfortable going to different meetings and events by yourself, make a plan to do it anyway. But make it more enjoyable by going with a friend. Once you get to know a few people, you will feel more comfortable going back on your own.

You can also begin with events that feel less intimidating. Sometimes the business-networking groups feel very serious—you must stand up and introduce yourself and say why you are there. If that feels nerve-wracking to you, begin networking by going to casual networking lunches or happy hours. Or go to an alumni group from your college or university where you will have something in common with everyone right off the bat.

Because one of the primary goals of networking is to meet people who can refer clients to you, we will get into networking in more detail in Chapter 13. Let's consider how to remove the discomfort and add the enjoyment into a few more high-impact marketing strategies for coaches.

### *Passive Marketing Strategies*

In addition to the active marketing strategies, you will want to rely on several print and audio products to serve as marketing and as revenue generators. Passive marketing can reach large audiences, can utilize the vast potential of the Internet, and can be done in your spare time. You can write an article in five days during your lunch breaks at your full-time job, while your baby is napping, or before you begin your day in the morning. Let's first talk about writing for marketing and then how you can market and make money at once. Now that sounds fun!

### *Articles and E-Zines*

Have an article idea? Why not share it with the world? You can do so by writing and publishing your articles. If you don't have any article ideas, do something easy like "The Three Steps to . . ." or "Top Mistakes with . . ." and fill in with something related to your coaching niche. Or have someone interview you about some topics related to your coaching.

Not a writer? Have someone write the article for you. You can do a search on the Internet for a ghostwriter. Or you can join an online group for coaches and then ask the group if anyone has a good ghostwriter or copywriter who writes in a similar niche.

Once you've written a compelling article, you can publish it in places like:

- Your company web site.
- Other company web sites.
- Professional journals.
- Newspapers.
- Local free magazines.

- Your newsletters and e-zines.
- Other company newsletters and e-zines.
- Online through article distribution and e-zine content sites, such as Ezine Articles at http://www.ezinearticles.com or Idea Marketers at http://www.ideamarketers.com.

If you really do not like writing but want to publish a great e-zine with coupons and other incentives for people to learn more about your coaching, you can obtain the articles from elsewhere. Of course, it's best to write your e-zines yourself because only you can best convey your ideas, value proposition, and information. If you are not a writer, however, do not let this stop you from publishing an e-zine. You can search online for free content by doing a search on Google. com. You can also write your own material and get an editor to go over it, tighten it, and correct your grammar. Search on terms like *copy editor* and narrow the list to your coaching niche.

You might also like to check out Customized Newsletter Services at http://www.customizednewsletters.com/, which provides excellent e-zine services for coaches and consultants who, for whatever reason, cannot or won't write and distribute their own newsletters.

### *Advertising*

You'll find many great tips for how to use advertising effectively in Chapter 16. Here we just want to point out that advertising can be relatively stress-free (except the paying for it part) and that watching the results roll in (when you do it right) is exciting. Don't even considering advertising if you can't run more than one ad. Remember that it takes several advertisements to generate action. People need to see marketing about five times before they are ready to act on it.

Also do not expect things from advertising that it cannot promise. In reality, advertising doesn't have the power of active strategies because it doesn't help people know you. Imagine the impact, however, when it's combined with other strategies. Someone in your local area hears you on the radio and is impressed with what you have to say. Then, two days later, they see your ad in the newspaper with your telephone number and office address. It feels like fate, and your number is right there, so they pick up the phone and call.

## *The Joy of Passive Income!*

The three of us have been using passive income-producing strategies for some time, very successfully, and Larina Kase has a great story to share with you to illustrate how it works. Larina just began generating passive income a couple years ago, and now she's a true believer of the beauty of it. One day over the holidays in 2004, she was skiing in Vail, Colorado. She went online and found she had earned $450 while skiing that day! She then had dinner and checked again—she'd earned $90 more. How fun is that? And Terri Levine and Joe Vitale have been enjoying massive incomes for some years now from passive sources they've created. So you see, when the experts are doing something easily and successfully, you know it is definitely something worth doing yourself. We are all enjoying profits from passive income sources, and you can take it from us . . . it's the only way to fly!

Not only is it exciting to have money coming in while you are out doing other things, but when you create a great product that you feel proud of, it's wonderful to think that people are out there reading it, listening to it, watching it, and benefiting from it. And they are benefiting from something you did several days, weeks, or months ago.

Another great thing is that you can reach more people with your products than your services. Most people can afford a $19.95 or $29 e-book. Many people cannot (or feel they cannot) afford your coaching packages at $500 per month. With your products, you help more people. And helping people is why most of us got into coaching in the first place. There's the joy!

*And* if all that isn't enough, products are great marketing tools. Let's say that someone looks on your web site and is interested. They aren't sure about coaching, so they order a CD that you sell on your site. They listen to it while they are driving, and by the time they get home, they are so interested in what you have to say that they call to schedule a free coaching session or initial consultation that you offer.

When you use affiliates, it becomes even more enjoyable. People are out there selling your products or services for you. You give some sort of referral fee, commission, or other benefit (keep in mind that you can't pay fees in many professions like healthcare and finance), and your affiliates are motivated to refer people to your web site. When you generate traffic, you look at your web site statistics and see the chart of visitors peak. How cool is that?

*Publicity*

Publicity is getting your ideas and name out into various media, like television, radio, magazines, web sites, and newspapers. You may pay a publicist to help you get the placement, but you do not pay for the placement yourself, that would be an advertisement.

One of the entertaining things about publicity is seeing yourself in the media. It is neat to have someone call you and tell you they saw you in *The New York Times*. If you want PR to be enjoyable, then be selective about which media outlets you are seen in. We've found a direct correlation between the quality of the media and the accuracy with which we were quoted. You have probably noticed this; the accuracy of statements in some gossip magazines is often more questionable than statements in reputable magazines. Finding a horrible misquote is disturbing and potentially harmful to your image. The higher-quality media fact-check your background and statements.

To generate publicity, you can do your own or hire a publicist. There are a variety of ways in which publicists charge for their services. Some charge you a monthly retainer, and others like Annie Jennings PR charge for placement.

### Annie Jennings Interview

Annie Jennings PR created her national Pay for Placement Publicity Program to allow everyone access to media placements without the high cost of monthly retainers. You pay only for secured media placements that actually air or print! Thousands of experts have booked their media placements using this innovative program. Please contact Annie Jennings at 908-281-6201 or annie@anniejenningspr.com.

**Anyone who has heard your teleseminars or met you knows that you are about having fun with marketing. Why is publicity so much fun?**
Actually, I am about serious marketing, I just happen to have fun doing it. Why? Because I love what I do! I love the thrill

of the chase. So going after a media placement for me is serious fun! That is why I have learned the fastest way to a media placement and have developed the most cutting-edge publicity strategy designed to land the media placement *fast!*

To have great fun when pursuing the media, I recommend having your publicity materials prepared professionally either by yourself (after you have learned about how to create a segment-style press release and the other essential PR tools) or by a professional publicist. The media can spot an amateur fast, and the media prefer to use a seasoned expert or one that appears to be a high-quality expert. Poorly prepared publicity materials or untrained publicity skills negatively mark the newbie. There is lots of competition for the media placements, so high-quality, professional presentation to the media gives you the edge.

### How have you seen life coaches or executive coaches effectively use the media?

A life coach or executive coach can be in great demand by the media if they are developed; that is, they have various interesting topics they can discuss that reflect the interests and concerns of our society. The more credentials you have, the better your credentials help identify you as a top expert, and a strong platform will position you favorably with the media.

Who is in a better position to personally experience the challenges people or executives face than a life or executive coach? Coaches are in the real world. If they can turn their firsthand knowledge into story or segment ideas, they will be sharing "next-level" ideas or the "next big thing." And what is the media always looking for? Exactly that!

Coaches are in demand if and only if they are on the cutting edge with the "next big thing" always developed and ready to go. Coaches should know the problems and the solutions of their audience and be able to turn their experiences into segment and story ideas.

*(continued)*

**What are your top five tips for what coaches need to do for maximum exposure?**
Here are five tips for maximum exposure:

1. Start an e-mail or e-zine newsletter.
2. Buy a media database so you know who to contact.
3. Learn publicity skills, including how to develop a segment or story idea and build a powerful platform.
4. Pitch the same targeted media contacts consistently over time with new, next-level, intriguing ideas.
5. Be sure to have an online media kit and media web site.

**How can coaches sign up to be one of the experts in the Pay for Placement Publicity Program?**
You can become an expert at http://www.anniejenningspr.com/experts.htm.

Another PR strategy is to submit press releases to various media outlets. With the help of the publicist, you can submit releases to newspapers. But why pay a publicist? You can submit releases yourself to local media outlets. You can also submit your releases to online resources like PR Web Press Release Newswire at www.prweb.com, which distributes them for you. Larina once submitted a release on that site that was viewed more than 15,000 times. She spent only $80 for this exposure. It is a valuable source that we use and recommend. Publicity is one of the best ways to build your coaching business because it gives you instant credibility. Learn more about using publicity with Terri Levine's tips on free PR in Chapter 16.

## Marketing Buddies

Still looking for ways to make marketing more enjoyable? Why not pair up with others and help out each other? You will learn from one another's experiences. This will help you save money because you can learn from your friends' mistakes as well as your own. Of course, you will also learn what works and do more of those marketing tactics. Having a marketing partner will help you effectively utilize professional relationships. You will be able to give each other support.

You can find amusement in your chats together and laugh about your different experiences. If you have one of those situations in which everything goes wrong and it feels like a comedy of errors, you can gain comfort in knowing that you will soon be laughing about it with your friend.

What if you and your friend are like the blind leading the blind? Then it is less likely to be effective. But, you can get help. You can both hire your own business coach. Then you can get together to compare the things you came up with when you had a session with your coach. You will be getting the benefit of two great coaches for the price of one. If you are strapped for cash, you can hire one coach and share the costs. For example, if you will be the one working with the coach, you can split the fees 70-30 with your friend because you can then help your friend with all the ideas you come up with when working with your coach. Your friend will get the benefit of the coaching for only 30 percent of the cost. Another option is what Terri calls *duo coaching,* and she does this for small-business partners. It involves you and your partner being coached simultaneously. It's very effective, cost-efficient, and time-saving.

So, set up weekly marketing buddy meetings, create a plan for active strategies, start writing your articles and creating products right now, and start enjoying your marketing. It really is fun, and it will bring you more opportunities to do what you love—coach!

# 12

# Effective Proposals, Projects, and Joint Ventures

*The successful always has a number of projects planned, to which he looks forward. Any one of them could change the course of his life overnight.*

—Mark Caine

## There's More to a Successful Coaching Business . . .

. . . than your individual clients. Most successful coaches have multiple streams of income. They diversify their portfolios of business investments and business income. In addition to your regular individual clients, you can create products, projects, and joint ventures. You can write proposals to get contracts that may involve things like speaking engagements, training sessions, or designing a curriculum.

Why are these multiple streams of income such a good idea? There are tons of reasons. Here are a few:

- Don't put all your eggs in one basket; diversify and lower your risk.
- Keep your energy level up for your individual clients. Don't burn out yourself trying to work with too many clients to make huge profits.
- Earn passive income so you can do two things at once. For example, you can earn passive income while speaking with a coaching client. This is virtually the only way we can literally be two places at once.

- Introduce your services to large numbers of people.
- Provide lower-cost services to people who may not otherwise be able to afford them because they get a bulk rate.
- Utilize the great sales potential of the Internet and affiliates.
- Find out where your true passion lies. You may think it is with coaching, but you may find that you love creating products and selling them online.
- Meet ambitious, fascinating, and inspirational joint-venture partners.
- Increase the likelihood of discovering the next big thing that will make you wealthy, famous, or booked with clients.

As you can see, we can go on and on. There are so many reasons that you want to get involved with products and projects. Convinced? Then here's how to get going.

## The First Step: A Compelling Proposal

Many great projects require a strong proposal. In fact, you may need to write a proposal for individual coaching clients as well. If a client's company is going to pay for the client to be coached by you, they often request a proposal. The company must be convinced that it will achieve a great return on investment by hiring you to coach their employees.

Whether you write a proposal to coach 1 person or 50, the format that you need to use is similar. These proposals also can be useful for getting training and speaking engagements. They can also work for making bulk sales of your books or other products.

As with all marketing, the key to a great proposal is to communicate "What's in it for me?" for the reader. Whoever is hiring you must be convinced that they need what you are selling. First, they will receive great benefit from the products or services that you offer. Second, they must be convinced that *you* are the best person to deliver the benefits that they need.

## What's in a Proposal?

The contents of your proposal are very important. Equally important is the way that you write. If you are not confident in your writing abilities, consider hiring a copywriter to help you write or a copy editor to edit your work.

In general, your proposal should include the following elements:

1. **Situation summary.** Describe here the current situation and reasons that people stand to gain from considering your proposals. This includes why the company or organization needs your services or products.

2. **Objectives.** Here you describe some of the ways in which you seek to help the organization. You identify the need and then position your products or services to fill the need.

3. **Description of your program.** Here discuss your coaching, training program, or products. If you are presenting a workshop series, provide the title and a brief description of the services provided (remember that you will focus even more on the benefits than the features; the benefits are described in the next section).

4. **Benefits of your program.** As you can imagine, this is the most important section of your proposal. You want to clearly delineate each specific benefit. You can use bullet points or numbers to further draw attention to each point. The more specific your benefits, the better. If you have data or statistics, that strengthens your points.

5. **Programs and pricing structures.** Although it is often not a good idea to include prices in marketing materials, it is often a good idea to include pricing in your proposal. Decision makers can become annoyed if they are given a proposal and don't know what they are looking at in terms of the financial investment. You can give a ballpark price and get into specifics later. A proposal is usually not the initial introduction to your services. You would typically introduce a proposal after some preliminary discussion. Always include this part in your proposal after your benefits because you want the benefits to be so strong that the price feels like no big deal.

6. **Your qualifications.** Don't be shy here. You need to fulfill the objectives described previously: They need to be convinced that *you* are the best person to deliver the benefits that they need. At this point in your proposal, the decision maker may be

thinking, "Wow, our sales force really could benefit from some group coaching." This is not enough for them to walk away from your proposal with because they need to think that you (or your company) are the one(s) whom they must hire.

7. **Testimonials.** To further show the readers why they would be crazy not to hire you, end the proposal with some testimonials from clients who hired you for a similar service. The more similar the services provided the better. If you do not have similar testimonials, then you can use more generic ones so the reader can see how well you help others. If you do not have testimonials yet, you can include published quotes about the benefits of the types of services you offer. It goes without saying that you should not make up testimonials. Remember the attractor factor: If you put out dishonesty, you are likely to attract it. If you have nothing to say for this section, then don't include it, just work on making your selling points in other parts of the proposal very strong.

## Projects for Passive Income

We've already talked about the joys of passive income. If you've created and sold products, then you know what we mean. For some reason, however, many coaches hesitate about selling products. This is often due to a fear of the unknown. The unknown is typically the technology and marketing involved.

Technophobia is a common fear. It taps into the fear of the unknown. The idea of needing to use technology to make your project successful can feel daunting and intimidating. Like any phobia, technophobia often results in avoidance. You sit down at your computer and feel that you do not know what to do (create a PDF file, update your web site, and so on), so you decide to come back to it later. Does this sound familiar?

As you know by now, avoidance is the food that feeds anxiety. The more you avoid technology, the more you will fear it. If you try to confront your fears and begin to educate yourself about the things that you do not know, you will find that it is not as threatening as you had assumed.

Myths about the technology necessary for creating and marketing your e-book are believed because they allow you to not work on your project. They serve as excuses or reasons to continue avoiding your Internet project. You tell yourself, "I don't really know how to do that yet, so I'll focus on other things." Holding onto misconceptions can be helpful when you want to procrastinate. It is much easier for me to say, "I should work on my e-book right now, but I don't know how to create a PDF, so I'll do it later" than to face my fear and get the answers to my questions and resolve my confusion.

### *Top Myths about the Technology Involved with E-Books*

For the e-book *What's Stopping You? How to End Self Sabotage for Aspiring E-Book Authors* (Wimberley, TX: Hypnotic Marketing, 2005), Joe Vitale and Larina Kase surveyed 349 participants about what keeps them from creating their product. They found that there are many concerns, questions, and misconceptions fueling technophobia and avoidance. The most common of these are myths about how hard it is to create or market the product.

Here are some of the misconceptions we found and Joe's responses:

1. *I need to become a real Internet marketing expert before I can sell my e-book.*

   I don't know any "real Internet marketing experts," and I (Joe) am considered one. You don't need to become an expert. You don't need to know much more than this: Who my audience is, where they are, and what they want. You then provide it to them. That's marketing.

2. *I need to know about all the Internet rules and regulations (which will take a long time to learn) like the Internet Compliance Act.*

   The Internet has no rules. The only thing you can't do is spam. And spamming is simply mailing to people who consider your e-mail junk e-mail. The only legal thing you must do is provide your snail mail address in all your outgoing commercial e-mails. That's it.

3. *I am confused as to the best e-book creation software. I think that I will need to buy Adobe, and I can't afford it.*

   The number-one format for e-books is PDF. The easiest way to turn a book into a PDF is to simply write it in Microsoft Word and then go to http://www.primopdf.com/ and use their free software to turn it into a PDF. Or sign up for a free trial on http://www.adobe.com. You're done. It's that easy.

The thing about technology is it is intimidating until you begin. Once you get started and tackle it step-by-step, it is simple. And if it isn't, you can hire someone to help you, or you can barter services with someone who can help you implement your product with the right technology. Or you can team up with someone and create a joint venture, which we'll discuss more in a bit.

### So What Should I Make?

The list of opportunities for products and projects is endless. The only limitations are your own creativity, knowledge, and skills. Here are a few ideas to get you started:

- An e-book on your area of expertise.
- An audio e-book.
- A brief e-doc as a how-to book.
- A series of e-docs that can be sold separately or together with a discount.
- An audio interview with a legend in your niche area.
- An audio that walks listeners through something step-by-step.
- A video from one of your speaking engagements.
- A bound set of training materials.
- A questionnaire or assessment or series of them.
- A published description of the results to a large survey that you conducted.
- A self-study coaching program.
- A self-study program that other professionals can use to receive continuing-education credits.

Still can't think of something to create? Why not find something out there that you love and ask the author if you can modify it for your target audience? You can then split the fees you earn 50-50, and it's win-win for both of you. Plus, you have met someone with whom you can do future joint-venture projects. This brings us to the next point.

## Joint Ventures: The Key to Success

We all love joint ventures (JVs)! This book reflects how much we love them because this book is a JV in itself. A JV is when two or more people or companies team up to create a unique product or program.

One of the best things about JVs is the quality of what you produce. Two minds are greater than one. When you have more than one set of ideas and perspectives, you are able to offer a lot more to your buyers. When your ideas converge with those of your JV partner, the ideas gain increased credibility. When you bring a different set of ideas and experiences, your clients and readers gain so much more from the service or product.

### *Joint Ventures for Stress Reduction*

With a business partner, your stress level goes down. You don't have to worry as much about mistakes in your product because you have two sets of eyes to look over everything. You have someone to bounce ideas off and from whom you gain inspiration and motivation. You automatically have a second opinion before you try something new. This enables you to take risks that can really pay off.

Your stress goes down when you know that you are creating something innovative and fantastic. You will have more ideas for marketing your product or services, and you will benefit from all of the marketing ideas and experiences of your JV partner. When you have complementary skills, you can rely not only on your JV partner to help with aspects that are not your strengths but you can also build new skills. You can learn from your JV partner and use the knowledge to create or market other products.

Of course, the workload gets distributed when you have a JV. It is great that you can still get credit, recognition, publicity, and income from something while doing half or less of the work. There are many ways to divide the work and the shares in the profits. The most common way is by the percentage of work that you will do. If you do 70 percent of the work, you typically receive 70 percent of the profits. Do not hold fast to this idea, however, because it is often a good idea to accept less than the amount of work you do if there are other significant benefits. If your JV is well known and will have the ability to sell a lot of your products or programs, then this gets additional value. Although you may do 70 percent of the work, if your JV partner has a large platform to help with sales, consider offering to split the profits 50-50.

### *Who's a Good Joint-Venture Partner?*

The answer is a personal one because it depends on what you're looking for. The key is for your JV partner to add something that you don't have. It should be mutually beneficial, and you both should gain from the partnership. It needs to be a situation in which the whole is greater than the sum of the parts. This is the idea of synergy. When you combine forces, something bigger and better results.

Here are some things to consider when looking for a JV partner. A good JV can be someone who:

- Is inspirational and motivates you.
- Has a great deal of skill and knowledge from which you can learn.
- Is fun and enjoyable to work with; someone you respect and like.
- Has a large platform and sales ability.
- Has innovative, unique ideas.
- Is dedicated to your project and gives it priority.
- Has other products that you can easily modify to create something new.
- Is serious about creating successful products or programs.
- Can significantly benefit from working with you.
- Is disciplined and reliable. They stick to their timeline (they give things to you when they say they will).

This last point is extremely important. As wonderful as JVs can be, they are only as good as the person you JV with. If the other person is unreliable, the JV can become much more frustrating than it is rewarding. If they don't do the work they say they will, you end up doing more work than you had anticipated. If they don't get things to you on time, you can be held up, and all of your other work can suffer as your schedule falls apart.

---

**Interview with Milana Leshinsky**

Milana Leshinsky is the founder and CEO of the Association of Coaching and Consulting Professionals on the Web (ACCPOW) and the number-one provider of web-based tools for coaches at http://www.RichCoachPoorCoach.com.

---

**You have been very successful in joint ventures with other coaches and business people. What are some examples of them?**

    http://www.CoachingAssessments.com.

    http://www.ExtremeTechnologyMakeover.com.

    http://www.LicensingRevenueSecrets.com.

    http://www.CoachingBusinessPlans.com.

    http://www.Accpow.com/summit2005 and www.Accpow .com/summit 2006, an annual global coaching event based on JVs with coaching experts.

**In your work, you are an advocate for multiple streams of revenue and the product funnel. What are some ways that coaches can begin doing this?**

Creating a product funnel is very important because it not only makes it easier to create multiple sources of income but also allows customers with different budgets access to your information.

The best way to do this is by listing all the different problems your target clients are experiencing and interviewing people who specialize in solving them. This strategy creates instant audio products you can sell for $17 to $197 for the rest of your business life, if you choose so.

**How do you decide with whom to do a joint venture?**

A JV partner is great when:

- They possess expertise I don't.
- They have a large or highly targeted mailing list.
- They are known to be hardworking and have high integrity; in other words, they deliver!
- I enjoy working with them on a personal level (compatible business style, enjoyable personality, fun to work with).
- They appreciate me and what I can do for their business.

**If someone sends you a proposal for a joint-venture project, how do you evaluate if it is a good one?**

I visit their web sites and check out their traffic rankings on Alexa.com. It's important to determine how professional their

*(continued)*

site is because this tells me how serious they are about their business. I make sure their proposition is mutually and equally beneficial.

I also make sure their proposition will contribute to my business not only short-term but long-term. For example, affiliate commission is not of interest to me as much as being able to promote my product to their network and grow my database of customers as well as gain wider exposure.

**Why do you think that projects and joint ventures create such excellent opportunities for coaches?**
JVs are incredibly fun—with the right partner. That's first and foremost! Business grows and products are created much, much faster because you double your resources *and* keep each other accountable. (I created LicensingRevenueSecrets.com with Suzanne Falter-Barns in 30 days. It would've taken me months to do this on my own!)

It helps you create multiple sources of income (assuming you're cocreating a product) much more easily. At least 50 percent of my products have been cocreated with strategic-alliance partners!

# 13

# Larina Kase's Tips for Successful Strategic-Referral Partnerships

*I know the price of success: dedication, hard work, and an unremitting devotion to the things you want to see happen.*
—Frank Lloyd Wright

In this chapter, I am going to share with you many of the secrets that I tell my coaching clients about filling your business through referrals. After helping dozens of coaches and other service professionals create thriving businesses, I have found that the best methods are strategic-referral partners and public speaking. These methods also have worked for me. I find working with strategic-referral partners to be one of the most enjoyable marketing strategies because you get to meet and work with so many interesting and inspiring people! Once you get your referral partnerships going, they are easy and fun. So if you'd like to have a steady stream of referrals at all times, read on.

## What Is a Strategic-Referral Partnership?

In professional-service businesses like coaching, referral partnerships are one of the most effective ways to generate clients, if not the most effective way. A strategic referral partnership (SRP) is a win-win referral partnership with the goal of satisfying the client. It is a client-centered approach, and you only want to work with SRPs whose primary interest is in benefiting the client.

You would not want to work with an SRP who was only in it for the referral fees. Imagine yourself as the client. How horrible would you feel if you found out that someone you trusted referred you to another professional whom they didn't even know much about? You would feel awful! So if you are going to go the referral-partner route, you must take it on as your responsibility to learn about the referral partner.

In an SRP, partners either refer to one another or one partner refers to the other partner. For example, a business coach partners with an accountant. When one has a client who needs the services of the other, they will make the referral to the other. The coach and the accountant know the quality of each other's service and feel good about referring to the other. As the coach, it may even be your own accountant (who is wonderful!) with whom you get into a referral relationship. In the best-case scenario, the number of referrals that each partner makes to the other is relatively equal, so the partnership continues to feel mutually beneficial.

An SRP can also involve one party referring to the other without necessarily receiving referrals in return. This partner may receive a different form of benefit in exchange for the referral. The referral partner in this instance is not looking for referrals but can still enjoy the relationship. We'll get into some of the benefits you can offer your referral source later.

## What Can a Strategic-Referral Partnership Do for Me?

In a word, everything!

An SRP can fill your business. An SRP can give you instant credibility. An SRP can warm your prospects, making it easier for you to cold-call because the call becomes a warm call. An SRP can get you in front of prospects whom you wouldn't otherwise have the opportunity to meet.

Your SRP can be working for you while you're doing other things. As you're going about your day, your SRP is considering who would be a good referral for you. Doesn't this sound nice? We'd all like someone to help us. This is what SRPs do! They are qualifying your prospects for you. They are using their brainpower to help determine who is a good client for the services you offer.

As we have discussed throughout this book, targeting the right group of people is absolutely key in marketing. Your SRP will have access to your target market. They can then further qualify prospects within your target market to see who will be the perfect match. The SRP will refer the right clients to you. We don't want you to build just any coaching practice; we want you to build your *ideal* coaching practice. SRPs can help bring those ideal clients to your door (or telephone).

The marketing process is often characterized by the acronym AIDA, which stands for attention, interest, desire, action. The reason that I love using referral partners is because they jump-start your marketing process and bring people right into the sales cycle. Wouldn't you love to bypass all of these complex and costly steps and get people right into action? By describing your services and recommending them, your referral partner has already captured the prospect's attention, gained their interest, and stimulated desire. Companies spend hundreds and thousands of dollars to bring people to this point of the marketing cycle. But you don't have to if you build your SRPs the right way.

Once your prospects are through A, I, and D, all that is left is the second A: action. *And* if your referral partner tells the prospective client exactly how to get in touch with you and when to do so, even this last step is facilitated. Sometimes, when a credible source recommends something to you, the recommendation is all it takes to go out and buy it. There are some excellent marketing books that I recommend to my clients. Often, my client says, "Oh yeah, I've heard of that book. It's supposed to be great." Why haven't they bought it yet? Sometimes they just haven't had the impetus. Your SRP gives the prospect the impetus to enroll in your services or buy your products.

## Who Makes a Good Strategic-Referral Partnership?

To build your business using SRPs, it is crucial that you select the right ones. If the SRPs you go after are not ideal, you will be wasting your time and theirs. It will become frustrating and will defeat the entire idea of a referral partnership. Don't make this mistake. Choose the right ones!

Many of the points that make a good SRP are similar to those that make a good joint-venture partner, as we discussed in the previous chapter. These are things like respecting the individual or company's services, being able to learn from your SRP, and being similarly business-relationship minded. This last point is very important. Some people are more business and referral minded than others. There are some people who are very well connected in their communities and who enjoy setting up people professionally. These are the natural networking types. Surely, you've met some people like this. Referrals flow from these types of people.

You want someone who is an ethical businessperson as a referral partner. You will become associated with them, so be sure they are not doing things with which you don't want to be associated. Select people who are highly customer or patient focused, because they will want to help their clients get involved with other valuable services (yours!).

Be wary of people who seem desperate for clients of their own. First of all, they will not have enough people in front of them to select people to refer to you. Second, they are likely to be preoccupied with building their own business or practice and will be not thinking about you as much as you'd like. Third, there may be a reason why they do not have clients. Maybe they do not meet the requirements of ethical businesspeople that we described previously. Perhaps they are not well respected in the community. Unless you know these folks well and know the quality of their work, steer clear of those who seem desperate for business.

On the other hand, you don't want to select an SRP who is super-busy. Someone who is constantly running around is less likely to have you on their mind. They may not be motivated by the potential of cross-referrals from you because they're already booked.

Your ideal SRP is someone who is busy but not too busy. They have access to enough people to refer to you and are well connected. They are also thinking about getting their own referrals, which means that they should be thinking about giving referrals.

## Strategic-Referral Partner and Affiliate—Same Thing?

Strategic-referral partners and affiliates can be the same thing, but they are not always the same thing. Referral partners pass people to you and then you sell to them. They help you with your marketing cycle. They do this because they receive some benefit from the process of referring the prospect to your services. You, then, are responsible for actually enrolling the client in your coaching program.

Affiliates, on the other hand, are like salespeople. They sell your product or services for a commission, usually a percentage of the product they are selling. When an affiliate recommends your coaching services and gets a percentage of the fee when your client enrolls, they are acting as an SRP. There is some overlap between the two.

## How to Find Your Strategic-Referral Partners

The right SRP will differ for every coach. It depends on your niche, your goals, and your geographic location. Try this exercise: Brainstorm everyone who could potentially refer to you. You can do this list by professional titles or occupations of people.

To get you thinking about how to generate your list, here is a list of potential SRPs for someone who is developing a wellness-coaching practice:

- Health-club owners.
- Managers of spas.
- Owners of yoga centers.
- Homeopathic doctors.
- Chiropractors.
- Sports-medicine physicians.
- Physical therapists.
- Small-business attorneys.
- Small-business accountants.
- Owners of health-food stores.

Once you have your list, you want to decide who to target first. Identify which categories of SRPs have referred to you in the past. Think of to whom you have access and with whom you have credibility. Consider who would be most likely to send you the types of clients with whom you really want to work and can best help. Then select the top two or three potential SRPs from your list and begin there.

When I say two or three, I mean types of referral partners, not specific individuals. These are categories, like homeopathic physicians or divorce attorneys. You don't want to be all over the place in targeting SRPs for the same reason that you don't want to be all over the place in targeting clients: You will be spread thin and ineffective in all areas. Focus your efforts on one or two at a time. You can focus on three at a time if a similar thread exists between them, but be careful that you do not lose focus.

Once you know the type of referral partner you will target, generate a list of individuals who fall into those categories. If you have a connection to anyone, begin with them because they are already warm prospects to become SRPs. Go through one at a time. Call them and highlight a couple potential benefits to them or their clientele. Then ask if you can take them out to lunch to discuss a referral partnership opportunity. Most people will agree. If they say no, don't be shy to ask for the reason. This will help you shape your approach with other potential SRPs.

## Why Should They Refer to You?

Let's face it, everyone is superbusy and has a million things competing for their attention. Several of my coaching clients have gotten as far as identifying SRPs and even having a great meeting with them. They tell me how fun the lunch was and everything sounds great. *But,* no response. They wonder why nothing happens.

Want to know why? It is likely one of three reasons:

1. You didn't convince them of the value of what you offer.
2. You didn't give them a proper incentive or understanding of the benefit of referring to you.
3. You didn't give them a way to remember you.

## Your Value Proposition

When you meet with a potential SRP or any prospect, it is very important that you communicate your clear value proposition. If you hear someone describe the work they do, which sounds more compelling:

"I help people build their businesses by creating and using strong marketing strategies."

"I help people use the psychology of effective marketing so they stop wasting time and money and start getting clients now."

There isn't a huge difference, but there is a subtle difference in terms of the value that is communicated. The second statement is one of the value propositions of my business coaching. Because my background is in both psychology and marketing (which, of course, are closely related because good marketing is all about psychology), it would be unwise to not convey what makes my services unique.

Your value proposition is related to your unique selling proposition. It shows the unique value that you can offer your clients. This is so important to an SRP because the SRP must feel comfortable and confident that the services they refer to are top rate. I personally do not refer to services that I have not either tried myself or become convinced of their value. Your integrity and reputation are on the line when you make referrals.

As a side note related to this point, you may have seen the very effective e-mail campaigns that offer tons of free benefits and gifts when you make a purchase. For example, when you buy an e-book, you get 20 additional free gifts. These campaigns work very well. If you choose to do this to sell your products, be sure that your referrals for free services and products are top-notch. The purchaser of your product will look at those gifts as an extension of you because you gave them. If they are not created and delivered by credible sources, your reputation could suffer. And you could miss out on one of the most important reasons that coaches sell products: potential new clients.

Your value proposition shows the benefit to the client whom the SRP refers. Once the value is clear, the next step is to motivate the SRP to refer by making the benefits to them explicit.

## The Benefits of the Strategic-Referral Partnership

If you are looking for an SRP to refer to you, it is critical that you know what is in it for them. This will give them incentive to think of you and refer to you. As with any form of marketing, the primary question is "What's in it for me?" The referrer will be motivated to refer to you when the benefit to them is crystal clear.

Another reason that clarifying the benefits is so important in helping someone refer to you is that they need to remember you. Most professionals are extremely busy, and although they may genuinely *want* to refer to you, they often simply forget. One of the best ways to get them to remember you is to create a clear benefit to them. There are some other ways, too, which I'll reveal later.

The benefits to the referring partner will change based on the nature of the referral relationship. To get you thinking, here are some examples of the common benefits:

### Referral Fees

In some industries, the referring individual can receive a referral fee just for referring to you. As you probably know, this is not the case in most health-care or licensed professions. Professionals such as physicians, psychologists, attorneys, accountants, and financial planners cannot receive a referral fee for sending a client to you. In business and other industries, however, referral fees are relatively common. If you are thinking about using a referral fee as your SRP incentive, be sure to take the steps necessary to insure that it is legal and ethical. To find out who can receive a referral fee, you can contact the state board of your profession and the referral partner's profession.

As far as things go right now, referral fees are acceptable in coaching and consulting. I know many top coaches who routinely give and receive referral fees. To determine how much of a referral fee to give, ask yourself what the referral is worth to you. Then give a referral fee around 20 percent. If you are giving a referral fee for a coaching client, you may want to give a flat fee rather than a percentage to simplify things. You can also stipulate that the fee is for new clients who enroll, not one-time coaching sessions.

Of course, there are many benefits that you can offer to those who cannot accept referral fees or if you don't want to give a referral fee. Psychological benefits are always powerful.

### Psychological Benefits

The psychological benefit comes from knowing that you have a high-quality referral source for your client or patient. Have you ever had that experience of feeling really good after giving someone a referral for something that you truly believe will help them? Think about a time when you found a client a good psychiatrist, physician, nutritionist, or chiropractor. Doesn't it feel great to be in or refer someone else to trusted hands? It is also marketing by giving; often what you give will come back to you.

It feels great to know that you have this SRP to make your job easier and to make you more effective. It also builds credibility to offer high-quality referrals. It shows that you are well connected and that you know your field and know your craft well.

To use the psychological benefits as the referral incentive, your value proposition, expertise, and credibility all must be excellent. And you have to do a great job of communicating all of these things to the SRP. One way to do this is by giving the SRP some specific examples of how you have helped people in the past. You can do this with case studies and testimonials.

### *Cross-Referrals*

The easiest and most straightforward type of referral partnership is one in which you both refer to each other. You refer to your SRP with the understanding that they will refer to you as well. You have an SRP and you are an SRP.

## How to Get the Strategic-Referral Partner to Remember You

As I mentioned before, your SRP may have the best intentions of referring to you, but they don't, simply because they are too busy and don't remember. You will not be the number-one priority in the mind of your potential SRP. Sorry, but it's true. They think you're great, and 30 minutes later, they've forgotten about you. If you are or have been an SRP yourself, you know what I mean.

One of the best ways to be memorable right off the bat is to communicate your powerful value proposition. If you sound like everyone else, you won't be memorable. If what you do and how your clients benefit sound different and intriguing, you will be memorable. Here are some more tips.

### *Keep-in-Touch Campaign*

The keep-in-touch idea is true for any type of marketing. This is why people create e-zines and newsletters. It keeps you alive in the minds of your clients, prospects, or referral partners.

You can create a separate e-zine or newsletter just for your SRPs. You can send them articles that are relevant to their clients or patients. These can be distributed electronically or through hard copies. Periodically, send little things, such as business-card magnets with calendars and some more brochures in case they run out. Don't forget to include your contact information on everything.

Why not create a special gift for your SRP to hand out? I would love anyone who helped me effortlessly improve the quality of the services I offer to my clients, and this would definitely get my attention.

### Frequent-Referrers Program

Are you like me, a sucker for those cards on which they punch off six items and you get the seventh free? I love those cards. My friends make fun of me because I get all excited about getting a free slice of pizza after buying 10! If you are trying to decide between two places to have lunch, that card in your pocket can be the tiebreaker. Likewise, if someone is trying to decide to whom to refer, the referral card make the difference.

The same idea can work for your referral partners. For those who can accept gifts, you can create a frequent-referrers program. For three referrals, they get a specific gift, like a free coaching session or packet of movie tickets. If they give six referrals, they get a bigger gift, such as dinner at an exclusive restaurant or an airline ticket upgrade. Or after six referrals, you give a free gift of coaching (a series of three sessions or a couple months' coaching) for them to keep or give to someone.

You can offer something for them and something for their clients as well. Their clients can get a free copy of your book or CD. People love free stuff. And free stuff helps market your coaching business. Now that's win-win!

The main point behind a frequent-referrals program is that you greatly appreciate the referrals and are particularly appreciative to those who send you several referrals. These are the referral relationships to nurture and build.

### Follow Up, Follow Up, Follow Up

One of the most important aspects of creating a referral partnership is follow-up. This is similar to keep-in-touch marketing and also serves the purpose of remaining in front of the SRP. It also adds an additional layer to the process because you will show them just how effective your services are.

With the client's permission, you can follow up with the referral providers to let them know how your client is doing. This will greatly assist with your ability to show your value proposition, and if the referrer is still working with the client, it can improve the quality of work they do with the client.

For example, one of my clients is a wellness coach. Chiropractors serve as a major referral source for her. The chiropractors are able to offer a more holistic approach to their clients. The coach gets written permission from her clients to coordinate services with the chiropractor. She sends the chiropractor a monthly update about the client's accomplishments and changes. The chiropractor is pleased to hear about these achievements. He is then eager to refer more clients to the coach.

## Become a Great Strategic-Referral Partner Yourself

The last point that I'd like to make about creating successful strategic-referral partnerships is to become a wonderful referrer yourself. You probably all know about the power of getting back what you give. As Joe Vitale says in his book *The Attractor Factor*, focus on what you want more of and give from the heart. If you want referrals, give referrals. But don't give referrals just so you get referrals back; give them because you really want to. Give them for the services that you believe in and want more people to benefit from.

When someone receives a referral from you, they are grateful. When you are appreciative, you want to help the person who helped you. This is just human nature. Think of the last time someone did something truly nice for you. What happened? Likely, you were thankful, and then you thought about what you could do for them in return.

*And* giving a referral helps you with your keep-in-touch campaign. You will be in touch with the referral in a very memorable and powerful way.

## Now Go for It

If you want a thriving coaching business, set up strong strategic-referral partnerships and work hard to keep in touch with your referrers and keep them and the clients happy. Look for opportunities to give excellent referrals, even if it means doing some research to decide for whom you want to become an SRP. Be a great SRP, get a great SRP, and watch your coaching business grow before your eyes!

Before we move on, here's some advice from one of my colleagues, Stephen Fairley, to give you a few more ideas about using SRPS.

### Interview with Stephen Fairley

Stephen Fairley is the CEO of the Business Building Center, http://www.BusinessBuildingCenter.com. Contact him at Ste.phen@BusinessBuildingCenter.com or 888-588-5891.

**As you describe in your best-selling book Getting Started in Personal and Executive Coaching, strategic-referral partnerships (SRPs) are one of the best ways to build a coaching business. What are some steps people can use to create effective referral partnerships?**

A strategic-referral partner is someone who already does business with or already has a relationship with the people you want to coach. The first step is to be absolutely clear about who is your best referral source. For example, many small-business coaches mistakenly believe accountants are their best source of referrals. However, because many other business coaches also target accountants, this is often not the case, especially in highly competitive markets. The first person or profession that comes to mind who could be your referral source is often not the best one. You need to test your ideas. Second, be absolutely sure the people you are trying to partner with are hungry. You want to approach only people who are actively trying to grow their business. If there is any indication they are satisfied with their current volume of business, move on. Last, do your best to make it a win-win situation. Offer to give them referrals or even a referral fee.

**How can you stay on the radar screen for your SRPs so they remember to refer to you?**

You should be in contact with your referral sources every 8 to 10 weeks. I'm convinced one of the biggest reasons why coaches don't receive more referrals is because they are not in regular contact with their referral sources. Here are some easy ways to keep in touch:

- Clip an article of interest to them from a trade magazine or newspaper.
- E-mail them an interesting article from a web site.
- Write an article they can pass on to their clients.
- Send them a couple copies of your new brochure.
- E-mail them a press release you wrote.
- Send them a card or small gift around the holidays.
- Meet them for lunch or coffee.
- Call them every time you have a referral for them.

**What are some of the mistakes you've seen coaches make in trying to establish good referral partnerships?**
The three most common mistakes are:

- Trying to obtain referrals from other coaches. Most of the time another coach is not a good referral source for you.
- Taking a random approach to referral marketing. Successful coaches take a systematic approach in which they actively target an industry or profession to build a referral network.
- Not designing the relationship to be win-win. For any referral relationship to work over the long term, both parties must receive some benefit from the relationship.

**What resources do you recommend to coaches to assist in their networking or creating referral partnerships?**
Business Network International is probably the best organization out there in terms of creating referral partnerships (http://www.bni.com).

# 14

# Joe Vitale's Secrets to Mastering Internet Marketing

*The secret to marketing is getting out of your ego and into your prospect's ego.*

—Joe Vitale

One day, my friend Bill Hibbler, an online coach and marketer, challenged me to write an article titled "How to Turn Personal Experiences into E-Books." He had seen me turn everything that ever happened to me into a book, audio, video, or e-product and then sell it online for a nice profit. He thought the idea itself could make money.

For example, Bill had been present when famous musician Pat O'Bryan walked into a meeting one day and jokingly said he wanted to write a book about the myth of passive income. Pat had been working night and day on his web site and didn't think there was anything passive about making money online. His comment was meant as a joke. I didn't think it was funny. I thought it was a product. That became an e-book we now sell at http://www .mythofpassiveincome.com.

The same thing happened 30 years ago when someone in one of my writing classes said they didn't have time to write a book. That led to me teaching a seminar on how to write your own book in six days. And that led to the record-breaking best-selling e-book Jim Edwards and I wrote on how to write your own outrageously successful e-book in less than seven days, at http://www.7dayebook.com.

Months ago, Amy Janota came to visit me. She had no idea how to make any money online but heard I had been doing it. She was broke. She wanted help. As we talked, I heard that she had taught herself how to play the guitar in two days. I recognized a product. She turned that into an e-book, which someone later bought from her for $10,000.

When my wife Nerissa and I bought a little James Bond gadget that could take video and photos and record audio, I had no idea what to do with it, whereas she had nonstop ideas. I told her to write a book on 101 ways to use your camcorder. It's now available at http://freevideoediting.com/camcorder.html.

When popular Las Vegas hypnotist Scott Lewis and I were sharing our excitement for the glitter and gold of Vegas, I suggested we write a book about their marketing secrets. It's now available at http://www.impulseinternetmarketing.com.

When my late ex-wife told me she wanted to find a way to get more money into her life, I thought about her love for makeup. Her favorite quote was, "Great hair, great day." She collected makeup like other people collect stamps. I urged her to write an e-book on the subject. She did. It's still for sale at http://www.mrfire.com/beauty.html.

I could go on and on. Bill was right. I can see opportunities everywhere. People who hang around me for even an hour often walk away with an e-product idea I spotted. I don't mean this to sound like bragging but to illustrate a point for all coaches.

For example, one night we had dinner with a musician and a writer. The musician just wanted to write music. The writer just wanted to write children's stories. They didn't see a match, let alone a product.

"Why don't you combine talents and create a multimedia e-book for kids?" I asked. "She writes the story, and you write the music. Kids can play it on their computers, reading along, listening to the music, and turning the pages with a click."

His eyes bulged, and he said, "How did you do that?"

"Do what?"

"Come up with that idea."

"I see them everywhere," I said.

And I do. Whenever someone says they have a problem, I hear an opportunity. When someone complained that they had to type their e-mails, I found a software developer and created Speak and Send, a program that allows you to talk your e-mails.

I'm not special. I used to *not* come up with ideas. But now, I see them all the time. I'm like the famous old headline that said, "Everywhere I stick my nose, I make money!"

So what happened to me?

All I did was decide to be alert for ideas. I started to read about people who came up with ideas. I started to pay attention to other people's products. And I made up my mind to turn on the inner radar. Because ideas are being spoken all the time — not blatantly, of course, but buried inside conversations — all I had to do was listen.

This very chapter is an example of what I mean.

Bill Hibbler challenged me to write this, and I did. It's yet another writing that came from direct life experience. You can do this, too. Any coach can. Turn on your mental radar. Become an idea detective. Stop hearing complaints and start hearing opportunities. They are everywhere.

I wasn't always like this, of course. I started online as an Internet skeptic almost 15 years ago. I didn't think you could make a dime online. Today, I'm one of the top 20 Internet marketers alive. I have more products than I can remember and make more money than I'll readily admit.

Speaking of money, let's pause and take a look at the numbers. Here's just a little proof of what you can earn selling digital information:

- The late Corey Rudl made $400,000 from his e-works.
- Stephan Mahaney made $800,000.
- Michael Campbell made $10,000.
- David Garfinkel made $35,000.
- Larry Dotson made $5,000 in less than a month.
- Allen Says made $15,000 on a Sunday.
- Bob Gatchel made $30,000 in one weekend.
- John Reese made $1,230,000 in one day.
- Tom Pauley made $250,000 in a year teaching the same e-class.

My own Hypnotic series of e-books, all e-published by Nitro Marketing, have broken sales records and left most of my printed books in the dust:

- *Hypnotic Writing* has sold in the tens of thousands—at $29.95 each—for more than six years now.
- My follow-up e-book, *Advanced Hypnotic Writing*, has sold well into the thousands.
- The e-work by Larry Dotson and me, *The Hypnotic Writing Swipe File*, came out of the gate with a bang, selling at the whopping price of $197 per copy.

And keep in mind that these e-books have no printing or shipping costs associated with them. They are invisible books. You don't have to warehouse them, either. When they sell for $29.95 or $197, that's virtually all profit. (A very nice feeling.)

I don't blame you if you are skeptical. I was, too, at first. Mark Joyner, the now retired CEO of Aesop Marketing, begged me for two years—*years!*—to give him a book of mine that he could release as an e-book. I'm a book lover and never thought anyone would ever buy an e-book. (So much for me being a futurist.)

But apparently there is an entire world out there—or online—that doesn't mind digital books and loves instant information delivered with a click. My *Hypnotic Writing* e-book sold 600 copies within 24 hours. I'm now a believer in e-books and all other digital products. They've enabled me to live in the beautiful Texas Hill Country, drive two luxury sports cars, own a heavenly pool, and travel as I please. Life is good.

My friend David Garfinkel, copywriting coach, grew up in the traditional publishing world and, in fact, worked for McGraw-Hill, the world's largest publisher of business information. He didn't give e-books much thought either until he released a couple of them himself. His most recent one is titled *Advertising Headlines That Make You Rich*. David told me, "I'm astonished by the results. I can honestly say my life has undergone quantum changes for the better in many ways since my first e-book hit the Internet a year and a half ago."

Of course, at this point in my career, I have dozens of e-books, e-audios, e-courses, and more. I also have software, from *Hypnotic Writing Wizard* to *Speak and Send*. And I didn't stop there.

On October 12, 2004, I released *Hypnotic Selling Secrets,* a giant home-study course compiled of old material, new material, and what-ever else I could find or create. With an orchestrated marketing campaign, and despite personal tragedy and awful technological malfunctions, I sold more than $450,000 worth of product in only three days. The site selling it became the 800th most popular site in the world on October 12. It's still up at http://www.HypnoticMarketingStrategy.com.

So, can you as a coach make money online? Of course. Here are some tips on how to do it:

### 1. Consider Your Expertise

You are probably a coach focused on serving particular clients. What are their current problems? What do they come to you to solve?

That's the first clue to what sort of web site or e-book you will develop.

### 2. Write an E-Book

Write an e-book that answers the common problems people hire you to help solve. Don't fear writing. You can speak your chapters and later transcribe them. You can even go to http://www.elance.com and post a job, saying you are looking for a ghostwriter to write the e-book for you.

### 3. Put Up a Web Site

Create a site that sells or gives away your e-book. It really doesn't matter which way you go because the idea is to use your e-book as a lure to bring in new clients for your coaching services.

In other words, if you focus on helping people overcome self-sabotage, you might have a web site titled *Overcoming Self-Sabotage.* When people search for solutions to self-sabotage, they may arrive at your site. This is where you want to capture their e-mail address so you can begin a relationship with them.

This is all so easy that it almost seems obvious to me. Yet I still hear excuses. Because of this, Larina Kase and I wrote a book on overcoming excuses for e-book authors, which is available at http://www.EndSelfSabotage.com. Some common excuses we've heard include:

*"I don't have a mailing list. Who will I mail anything to?"*

No one has a list when they first start. You can rent one. You can begin one by offering to send out a weekly tip, insight, or even a joke. You could even create an e-book and give it away, saying it's free in exchange for an e-mail address. Customers get a product, and you build your list.

For example, when Pat O'Bryan created the "Think and Grow Rich Workbook," he wanted to sell it. I suggested he give it away. That's how he built his own mailing list from nothing to 6,000 people. When Pat decided to become a coach, he sent a short e-mail to his list, told them he was available, and got 20 clients overnight.

*"I don't know how to build a web site."*

You don't need to know. You can hire someone from http://www.elance .com, you can buy software to walk you through it, or you can get courageous and learn it yourself. I probably have more than thirty web sites online, but I didn't build *any* of them. I tried to learn years ago, but it wasn't fun. When it isn't fun, I pass.

Take a look at one of my new sites at http://www .HypnoticMarketingInc.com. It begins with a movie. I have no idea how to create that. But my webmaster, Charles Lewis, does. A key to success is delegation. No successful coach tries to be everything or do everything.

*"I don't know how to create an e-book."*

Again, you don't need to know how. You probably didn't know how to be a coach, either, until you got trained. But here are the basics:

1. Write (or hire someone to write) your book. It can be a simple research project, a short or long report, a collection of information searched and compiled from online sources, a public-domain document on which you comment, and so forth. The world is your oyster.
2. Save the file in Microsoft Word. This is the easiest file to convert into PDF, which is the format virtually all computer

users can read. You can do a search at Google.com to find free software that will convert your e-book from a Word file to a PDF file or sign up for a free trial at http://www.adobe.com.

3. If you want to sell your e-book, put it on http://www .Clickbank.com. This is one of the most popular sites for selling digital information. I have several e-books here, including http://www.attractanewcar.com.

4. If you want to give away your e-book, then simply set up a web site that basically says, "You can have this for free in exchange for your e-mail." Your web site can be a simple squeeze page, which means the site squeezes the information out of viewers before they can access it. If you have something people want, you can build a mailing list fast.

Again, all of this is simple. There are numerous books out there that walk you through all the steps, including the one Jim Edwards and I wrote at http://www.7dayebook.com.

Of course, you should also be thinking about marketing your web sites.

Most coaches have a bad attitude toward marketing. Their thoughts are rooted in cultural perceptions that money is bad or selling is manipulation. I say get past all that. Money is good, and selling is sharing.

You should be so in love with what you do that you can't wait to share with others who might want to hire you or buy from you. Marketing is basically sharing your love with those most ready to benefit from it. That's it.

Finally, I encourage you to think about doing unusual things, things most coaches may never have dreamed of trying. For example: Do coaching by e-mail. See clients by web cam. Conduct seminars online. Create your own blog.

Again, the Internet makes being a coach more effective and more profitable than anything else in history, so far. Think outside of the box, be willing to try new things, and always, always *have fun!*

# 15

# Making the Most of Limited Resources

*Choice, not circumstances, determines your success.*

—Anonymous

## No Time or Money?

So many people think that they never have enough time or money to do the things they want to do. Then it feels like you are always trying to do things that you do not have enough time or money to do. How frustrating this is! Let's look at these separately.

### There's Never Enough Time

Maybe you feel like you are constantly busy and always trying to catch up with what feels like five million tasks. You'll never find the time to work on your projects because of all the demands in your daily life. You feel overwhelmed. Having a 48-hour day sounds like a good idea to you.

You might feel this way if you have a full-time job or numerous family commitments. Sometimes you feel you have so much to do there is just no way you can find the time to squeeze in even one more tiny project, let alone starting and marketing a business!

Then you might consciously or unconsciously decide to put off your marketing efforts because it feels like you will not have time to prepare and put them into action successfully. If you feel this way, review the section in Chapter 9 on Time Management (pages 102–106) to take a close look at your use of time and what can help you improve it.

163

Most things are not exactly a waste of time, but some things are a poor use of time, and there is a difference. You should learn from the experiences and then move on. Have you ever had an afternoon when you planned to accomplish 10 things but only got to 4 of them? We all have. This can be very frustrating and can end up making you less focused and motivated. Instead of wallowing in how unproductive your day was, focus on all the little successes and wins you created, no matter how small.

If there truly is one thing that is a waste of time, it is allowing yourself to get caught up in or relive past mistakes and problems. You may think that you can never be efficient or successful or good at marketing (or whatever your most challenging task) because of a mistake or difficulty you had in the past. They are in the past. Wallowing in them now won't serve any useful purpose. Learn from them, let go, and move on.

This quote is a great illustration of this:

Finish each day and be done with it.
You have done what you could.
Some blunders and absurdities have crept in;
forget them as soon as you can.
Tomorrow is a new day.
You shall begin it serenely and with too high a spirit
to be encumbered by your old nonsense.

*—Emerson*

You may find you use the "there isn't enough time" excuse to procrastinate and put off working on your business or special projects. Maybe you hold misconceptions about just how much time is needed to create a successful business. Maybe you are worrying for nothing. We will go into more detail about these misconceptions so you can at least get your facts straight and stop using this as an excuse in your life.

### We Could Always Use More Money

Take a look at these three questions and answer them honestly:

1. Are you afraid to invest too much time preparing your business and marketing plan in case you don't have the funds to promote it?

2. Do you worry that you will need to spend a fortune creating a web site with all the marketing tools required to sell your services? And what if no one visits your web site or buys your services, and then you've wasted all that precious money?
3. Are you tired of struggling with financial issues and thinking that you should just save your limited funds rather than invest them in risky ventures?

If you answered yes to these questions, then it is likely that your fears related to money may be holding you back. Money is a real concern for many people and presents a convincing reason for self-sabotage.

When finances are tight, it is common and natural to operate from a position of fear. The problem is that the more you focus on something, the more you will experience it. Another way of saying it is your thoughts create your reality. If you think you don't have enough money, then you will experience not having enough money more in your life. Why do you think millionaires believe in thinking positively and living with abundance? Not only can you worsen your financial situation by constantly focusing on your lack, but this type of thinking will limit your confidence and creativity. Your courage to venture forth will fly out the window.

Most of history's successful entrepreneurs have one or more stories they tell about a turning point or decision point in which they had to go after something that was not easy. They say that the only reason they found success was because they accepted the challenge and the possibility of multiple outcomes. Sure, they could have made a bad decision and failed, but they made a right decision and succeeded. What do you think they focused on?

In other words, you need to be willing to take the odd risk in order to gain anything worthwhile. You need to be willing to fail in order to be successful. There are no guarantees in life, but you can swing things in your favor with the right techniques.

If your fears about money are preventing you from living your dream of being a top coach, then ask yourself whether you are willing to accept a risk. It can and should be a calculated risk that has potential payoffs and rewards. Nobody takes the type of business risk that involves jumping into situations blindly. You stack the odds in your favor as much as you can to give yourself every chance of success. But it's still a risk. But for that matter, so is crossing the road!

As with time issues, you may be overestimating the risks and costs involved in your project. Doing this contributes to procrastination and putting off doing what you could be doing to get your project moving forward.

Maybe you are one of those people who says, "I will start work on my project seriously just as soon as I have lots of money saved so I can buy the expensive technology I need and invest in a top-notch marketing and promotion campaign."

This sounds like a sensible idea, but it may take a long time, right? Maybe this idyllic time of plentiful finances may never happen, then what will you do? You could be waiting forever.

On the other hand, you don't want to start a business without some money saved. The number-one cause of small-business failure in the United States is undercapitalization. This means that most businesses do not have the proper savings to become successful.

One problem that can arise in a coaching business is that you become so preoccupied with making ends meet that you begin making sacrifices that are hard to recover from later. You never want to undervalue yourself or start chasing after dead-end projects that don't really excite you just because they can pay the bills.

If you need to wait a couple months to begin your practice so you have the savings to do it right, that is fine. Just don't wait too long and get caught up in the cycle of avoidance and procrastination that we discussed in Chapter 9. Many coaches also begin their businesses part-time while they are still working. This can work well *if* you don't push the coaching business to the back burner while everything else in life takes priority. If you want to be successful as a coach, then your business must be a priority, even if it's part-time.

## Now for the Good News

If all this talk about the money has made you nervous, rest assured, much of this stuff is really not that expensive and you don't need to work on it 24–7. In fact, there are a lot of misconceptions out there about how you need to use your limited resources and how much you will need to invest. Here's the straight scoop.

## Top Myths about the Resources Involved with Creating Businesses (and the Answers to Them)

1. *I will need to spend loads of money to set up PayPal or a credit-card service and an autoresponder.*

   Let us tell you, PayPal is free. Furthermore, many web-hosting services offer credit-card services for less than $30 a month. As for autoresponders, these range from free to $100 per year. One popular one is http://www.aweber.com. You can get all of these from one place: http://www.citymax.com. None of this constitutes a lot of money.

2. *Creating my business will take months or even years.*

   What are you trying to build here? Another Disneyland? You can write a business plan in one day. You can certainly write one in seven days. You can positively write one in a month. And with the tools, such as the tapes, CDs, videos, and kits available from places like http://terrilevine.com/products.htm, there are no excuses for not being able to start and continue with growing your business and marketing it successfully in a short time. Do the math. How many coaching clients will you need to be profitable? It may be as low as eight clients per week. You can get as many as this number relatively quickly.

3. *I need large blocks of uninterrupted time set aside to work on my project.*

   Maybe you do. Maybe you don't. Some people get up an hour earlier than normal to work on their project. Some people use their lunch breaks. Some stay up later after everyone has gone to bed. Others choose to give up watching TV or some other time-draining activity. Never forget, where there's a will, there's a way!

4. *Creating an e-commerce web site will be prohibitively expensive.*

   We've already covered this. You can get a site with http://www.GoDaddy.com for about $15. You can build one for *free* at http://www.citymax.com. If you want to hire a freelancer to create your site, there is so much competition these days that you can find a web designer with great experience who is not very expensive. You can post a free ad on http://www.craigslist.com and require respondents to submit a portfolio so you can select a great one. Or go to http://www.elance.com for freelancers.

5. *Piracy worries me; people will steal my ideas, and I will make no money from it.*

Between the three of us, we have dozens of e-books, special PDF reports, articles, and so forth on our sites and others and have been selling them for years and have never once seen or experienced true piracy. Our advice is to worry more about creating a product *worth* stealing. Besides, if someone steals your e-book, for example, look on the bright side and call it *viral marketing.* The pirate is doing you a favor. He is distributing your name to the world. That kind of publicity would cost you thousands of dollars in advertising and publicity. You're now getting it for free.

6. *I don't know what is important to buy, and I will waste a lot of money that I don't have in buying the wrong things.*

You don't have to buy anything at all. If you want, you can market your business with only e-mail. But to make things automated, you at least need a basic web site. Again, you can get that from http://www.GoDaddy.com for about $15. You can produce reports and e-book products for less than $100. These products take some time to create, but it is time that can have an excellent return on investment in terms of passive income and marketing your business.

7. *Let's pretend you would like to write an e-book to sell as a promotional tool for your business and market it on your web site, but the thought of having to register it or get an ISBN turns you off because you don't know the procedure. So, you avoid writing the e-book and waste valuable marketing opportunities in the process.*

Here's the good news. ISBN stands for International Standard Book Number. All printed books require them for tracking purposes. E-books, however, don't require them. Most e-books don't have them. Of course, if you really wanted one for your e-book, you simply go to http://www.isbn.com and fill out their forms to become a publisher. But we repeat, e-books do *not* need ISBNs. And now that you know that, you can get started on your e-book!

8. *You believe affiliate marketing is so complicated. You're not even sure what it means!*

Affiliates are simply *salespeople.* They sell your products for you for a preagreed commission or share of the cost of your book, which we believe should always be 30 percent to 50 percent. You can find affiliates as easily as you can find anything else on the Internet. Just go to http://www.Google.com and type in the word *affiliates*. You can also find your target audience and ask them if they are interested in selling your product or service for you for a commission. If they say yes, they become your affiliates. That's all there is to it.

9. *Developing a big enough e-mail list will take years, and with all those complicated antispam laws, is it worth the bother? It will be expensive to build my list and send the e-mails.*

You'll be pleased to learn that you don't need a big mailing list. A list of only 50 people who are really interested in what you have to offer and buy your products is more valuable than a list of 100,000 people who delete your e-zine each week without reading it and never buy a thing from you. All you need is a list of people who truly do want what you have to offer. These people are your true target audience.

One popular method used for building a list involves giving free gifts as enticements. This might be the e-book you are now going to write! You put it on your web site available for download and tell people they can download it for free in exchange for their e-mail address. The one thing you need to be careful with using this approach is that as far as the anti-spam organizations are concerned, this does not give you the right to keep e-mailing these people if they haven't given you explicit permission to do so. Providing their e-mail address for the simple purpose of having an e-book sent to them is not considered explicit permission.

So perhaps you could word it to indicate that you'd like their address so you can offer them other freebies in the future and to keep in touch, and in this way, they are aware you probably will contact them again. And if they don't want that, then they don't have to give their address, and they don't get your freebie. Or you can do what Terri Levine does, which is to invite people to sign up for her newsletter mailing list, and for doing so, she offers them a free gift, and then throughout the year she keeps offering freebies to keep her list happy and subscribed.

It is not expensive to develop and send your e-zine. Your hosting company may have a service that does this. There are companies like http://www.constantcontact.com that create templates and send out your newsletters and track the data for you. You can create a free blog and send links to the blog.

**10.** *There is so much market competition out there that my service or product will never stand out. What chance would it have?!*

Joe Vitale suggests that you think about this question: Are there any cookbooks out there? Silly question, yes. The shelves are weighed down with every kind of cookbook known to humanity! There are thousands of them, right? Do you think there will be any new ones next week or next month or even next year? Another silly question. Of course there will. And why? Because people are never satisfied. No two cookbooks offer the same recipes. There's usually a twist, and as we're becoming more health conscious, recipes are presented with more healthful ingredients.

The lesson you should have learned from this little exercise is that provided you are offering the public something they want or will want, it doesn't matter if it's already been offered and the market is flooded with similar products or services. If you can find a way to add a twist to yours, you will sell it. The thing with marketing is if you don't do it, somebody else will come along and beat you to it. They'll be laughing all the way to the bank while you sob into your handkerchief.

**11.** *I'll never find a niche market that is big enough for me to make money in yet small enough to stand out and be effective.*

This is a common worry for beginners. We know one marketer who made a half-million dollars selling one product to a list that contained only 450 names. He was successful because the people on that list were all in his niche. This was truly his target audience. The world is made up of niche markets; no two people are interested in the same subjects or products. Don't choose a niche simply because you think you can make lots of money from it. Make sure it is something you are passionate about or, at least, find interesting enough that working on it and in it will be pleasurable to you and you won't start self-sabotaging again!

You can search online and look for groups who would be interested in what you have to offer. For example, say you plan to write your e-book and want to be sure there is a market for it. Go to Google and type in the subject of your proposed e-book. Every result that comes back is a potential market for your e-book. You may even find potential affiliates in the list as well.

12. *It's too hard to reach my market. It will take me forever and I'll have to spend a lot of money. How do I find them or how do they find me?*

This is an easy one. Both Google and Yahoo have groups. Go to http://www.Google.com or http://www.Yahoo.com and find their "Groups" link. Click on it and then open the directory. When you find the groups you believe are your target market, join the groups. Participate in their discussions and become known to them. Be friendly. Don't spam. Don't immediately try to sell anything to them either—that would be a mistake. Wait until they get to know you and accept you as part of the group, then you can talk to them about other things. You can even create your own groups on Google and Yahoo if you want to. It's as easy as falling off a log.

### Now You See . . .

. . . that you don't need tons of money saved or time on your hands. There's no reason not to pursue your dream of becoming a top coach, enjoying your work, helping clients live better lives, and earning a lucrative income.

Want some more inspiration and ideas? Then let's go on to some other top marketing tips. In the next chapter, you'll find more of Terri Levine's top secrets for building a coaching business.

### Interview with Jeanna Gabellini

Jeanna Gabellini is known as the "Xtreme Abundance coach." She was one of the first (and the youngest) coaches to receive the master certification from the International Coach Federation. She teaches folks how to go big in their business without pain and with a ton of fun! Visit her web site at http://www.MasterPeaceCoaching.com.

*(continued)*

**What are some of the important success principles you have learned in your coaching career?**

1. Have relationships with people who think bigger than you do. They will expand your visioning and creativity as well as inspire you.
2. It can be easy to be successful. Now, this doesn't mean that you won't spend time building your business and systems, but if it's hard, you need to change your strategy.
3. You will find evidence to support whatever you believe. If you think it's hard to generate new business, it will be. You will collide with people, articles, and televisions shows all confirming that business is hard or slow. The opposite is true, as well. If you believe you will attract new business easily, you will collide with all sorts of evidence that it is true. And guess what?! You'll always have a full pipeline of customers.
4. Don't ignore people, systems, marketing, and so on that aren't working. If you notice something is producing less than satisfactory results, address a solution immediately. Do not tolerate anything that doesn't make your business a joy to work at.
5. Create your business in a way that delights *you!* You get to make your schedule, your fees, your focus, and only work with clients you enjoy. Do it your way and you will be happy. A happy person who loves their work always attracts business and is prosperous!

**Why do you love being a coach?**
It feels effortless. I like to talk, be in relationships, and inspire people to go big in their lives. I want everyone to experience joy on a daily basis. I'd coach for free, but right now I'm loving the abundance that it's bringing.

Being a coach gives you endless opportunities to create multiple streams of income. You can coach any topic, any client, in any structure you want. Coaching is an easy career to create total freedom. Oh, and did I mention how much I love coaching and facilitating by phone to people all over the world? That is effortless! A phone and good coaching skills together equal endless possibilities.

**What are some of the resources that a coach absolutely must have to be successful?**

A mastermind group to meet with on a weekly basis. I've been with the same group more than five years! They are a constant source of inspiration, accountability, coaching, solutions, and creativity.

Also, I believe great coaches have coaches. I use them to unravel all kinds of limitations. I want to be deeply happy and peaceful, not to mention have an abundance of dollars. I want someone in my corner helping me see what I can't see. I like seeing different perspectives and being challenged to be my most powerful self.

Marketing musts: An e-zine is one of the easiest and most fun ways to market and keep yourself in front of your audience. Relationships with other successful people who you ask to support your marketing efforts. However you choose to market, you must enjoy it, or the results will burn you out. If you're enjoying the marketing process, it will yield business. Every time my business partner, Eva Gregory, and I come up with a promotion that we think is wild and nutty, it works. We laugh ourselves silly with some of the one-liners we put in our ads.

If you focus on your business, it will give you what you want. If you're not creating goals and intentions beyond contentment, you'll just get what you get. I create goals on a yearly, monthly, weekly, and daily basis, and I write *everything* down. I post them on walls, mirrors, and my desktop. I make sure I am very clear on what I will achieve. This is the single most important action step anyone in business can do. Stay connected to your desires and only takes actions that delight you.

**What are some of the myths, misconceptions, or limiting beliefs about resources that a coach must have to be successful?**

Any thought you think that leads to you thinking there is a right way to get business is limiting. Any thought that leads to

*(continued)*

you thinking there is only a certain amount of money you can make in a certain time frame is bunk. If you think you have to have business cards, brochures, web sites, an e-zine, and so forth to generate business, you are misguided. I created a full practice in a few months because I was fired up. I had *no* marketing materials, no niche, no clue! I just was excited and talked my head off about the power of coaching. I was also not attached to getting clients. I wanted them, but my mission was to educate the public about coaching. My best marketing (even in the very beginning) has always been referrals. The one thing I always drive home with coaches (and any other business person) is to charge what feels good. Many people get stuck in their "Am I worthy?" belief and charge very little for their products and services. You can charge whatever you want (and I mean whatever!), and if you feel good about it, you will attract a client base that feels good about it, too. This whole topic gets me on my soapbox for hours. I should teach a class on it. :-)

### How can coaches create abundance when they begin with limited start-up resources?

All anyone needs is to start talking about what they do and what benefits folks will receive from it. You can do it in person, on the phone, and through recordings and the written word. You must become visible, even if it is one person at a time. I was running a cleaning business and coaching at the same time when I started. I had one of the oldest computers known to man and didn't know what e-mail was. I was very clear that I loved coaching, and I was going to claim clients I liked. I'd walk right up to people and say, "You know, we'd be a great team." Mostly, they'd say yes. Was I nervous about getting a "no"? Yes! But I kept at it anyway.

You must ask for support from anyone you like. Even those folks who say they don't know anyone who can help, I tell them to go meet new people. Scratch their back and they scratch yours. You don't need resources (although they are great!), you simply need to be clear on what you want and be proactive about it. Surround yourself with people who make sure you remember how powerful you are. I still call people at low moments and ask, "Would you tell me how great I am? I'm having amnesia right now!" It works wonders.

**How has your work with other coaches enriched your career?**
Trading coaching back and forth has gotten me through some of the roughest moments of my life. There are dozens of coaches who have supported Eva and me in the most magnificent ways. Coaches send us clients, they are loyal customers, they get us interviews, they give us bonuses to give away with our programs, they give us acknowledgments. I could go on and on. They have supported us to where we are today. People like Terri Levine and Sharon Wilson have done so many joint ventures with us that it seems like they are a part of our business. They are an incredibly valuable resource.

And not to mention the fact that my partner, Eva, is one of the biggest blessings of my life. We have created the most effortless partnership and business I can imagine. It is based solely on the principle of choosing joy and only taking inspired actions. Having her as a partner makes everything a party. I'll stop gushing because I could go on for a couple of pages, and she might be doing the same.

**In your opinion, what are the key ingredients that help a coaching business take off?**

Believe in you.
Action.
Support.
Fun.
Keep your eye on the goal, not your current reality.
Be accountable to somebody.
Create systems that work.
Be inspired. Read books, listen to audios, take classes, hang out with amazing people, see great movies, have a good coach. Anything that will keep you connected to your vision and your power.

*(continued)*

Hire people who are experts in their field to assist you. You should only be doing what you are good at. I'm good at coaching and teaching. I can write well when I'm in the mood. Otherwise, I hand it all over to someone else or I don't take action until I feel inspired.

# 16

# Terri Levine's Top 10 Marketing Secrets

*Without promotion something terrible happens . . . Nothing!*

—P.T. Barnum

*Forget shoulds, create wants.*

—Terri Levine

Over the years, I have developed and tweaked many marketing strategies guaranteed to boost business and profits. I have used these techniques to build million-dollar businesses, and I teach these techniques to my clients and students. It's not possible to cover *every* marketing technique in one chapter; if it were, there wouldn't be so many specialized books and programs on the topic!

Fact: Being a great coach, or a great whatever you are, is simply not enough. Having impressive credentials is not enough. You can be the best in the business, but if people don't know about you or how to contact you, where will your clients come from? How will they find you? *Why* should they hire *you?*

Let's start with so-called elevator speeches. Some marketers believe these are a waste of time. What *is* a waste of time is having only a few minutes to impress somebody you've just met and, because you are unprepared, it takes you too long to get your message across and, before you know it, time constraints have prohibited you from completing your dialogue and you've lost a potential client or referral.

You never know when an opportunity will arise when you can introduce yourself and your business. Busy people don't have time to sit and listen to you waffle on for 20 minutes about what you do. If you can bring it down to a sentence or two, using powerful imagery in your language, you can hold and sustain interest and perhaps be invited to tell them more. So, my first marketing tip for you is . . .

## 1. Develop a Strong, Unique Elevator Speech

Don't think of it as an elevator speech, think of it as a *value proposition.* In 15 words or less, try writing a description about what you do. Don't waste words on telling about yourself or your qualifications. Your elevator speech must quickly explain how what *you* do helps others. For example, what problems do you solve? Don't try to be all things to all people, and don't try to tell everything there is to know about you and your business. If you know the line of business the person you've met is in, you will know which of your services is likely to appeal, and you can modify your speech and focus on that. You can now market yourself in as little time as it takes to wait for a bus, ride an elevator, be introduced at a busy network function, and so on.

## 2. Target Your Ideal Client! Get a Niche!

You must avoid wasting money by marketing to the wrong people, so you must know who your target audience is. For example: Are you a career coach? A health and fitness coach? A lifestyle coach? Develop a niche, and from this you will know who your target audience is and you will know where to find your ideal clients. Think outside the box on this. Think globally, not locally. If you're starting out, go for the niche that feels easier at first, and as you gain experience, you can add more.

Once you have your niche, you can go after the clients who would be interested in your particular services. Don't think that by joining a coaching association that this alone will bring in the clients. It won't.

- Where can you find and reach your ideal clients?
- Where are they likely to hang out?
- What professional organizations, if any, would these ideal clients belong to?

- What journals, magazines, and newspapers are these clients likely to read? Subscribe to the same and write articles for them. (This is also the best place for your advertisements.) This will get your name in their faces and establish credibility. Writing articles is also a very cheap form of advertising!
- Attend related trade shows and network. (Have your elevator speech ready; you will meet many people and have only a short time to introduce yourself before they move on.)
- Look in your local city business journals. Do they publish a calendar of events? If you see a particular meeting advertised that looks promising, contact them and ask them outright what the focus of the meeting is, who is likely to attend, and whether your attendance would be beneficial.
- Do *not* sit in your office waiting for the phone to ring. Go out and meet people in your niche area. Even if you don't personally meet new clients, the contacts you make can be valuable. They can refer clients to you. You can participate in joint ventures. Word of mouth can bring you new business.

## 3. Follow the Money

If you are starting out or going through a difficult patch, you can earn some quick dollars by attracting more lower-paying clients. In the long term, however, this is not going to create wealth, and the quantity of clients needed for business growth will burn you out.

To skyrocket your business, you need to look for high-paying clients. Let's assume you are a general lifestyle coach, a niche that provides many possibilities for finding new clients.

Make a list of the professionals with high-level incomes who are likely to use your services. Lawyers? Doctors? Dentists? Managers and CEOs? For what services are they most likely to use a coach? You need to develop a niche to cater to this high-paying group if you want to attract them. (The struggling unemployed are unlikely to be able to pay you $500 to $1,500 per month for your services!)

Don't just pick a high-paying niche for the money's sake. You also need to enjoy working with your clients. Have a good think about which types of people you would really enjoy working with over the long term.

### Don't Devalue Yourself!

Even in a tough economy, don't be tempted to lower your prices and devalue your work. For one thing, it is not ethical for you to offer one price to one client and a different price to another, and you will *not* build a wealthy business and lifestyle if you give your services away for free.

Don't fall into the trap of thinking that offering complimentary sessions will bring in profitable clients. It doesn't work that way. What you *will* attract are freeloaders who will take the freebie and never see you again, *or* they will annoy you trying to make you bring down your prices. Highly successful professionals do *not* offer freebies. By not offering freebies, you won't attract people looking for free services.

Note: This is *not* the same as offering a free 5- to 15-minute session to help you and a potential client determine if you are a good fit and will work well together.

### Tip: Make Services Affordable without Lowering Your Price

You want to bring in more quality clients without reducing your fees. If they are interested but having trouble affording your products or services, ask them if they want you to assist them to finance it, interest-free. Work out a payment plan they can afford. It might be something like only $50 per week with the option to pay more when they wish. Many people agree to this because even though your product or service might be out of their immediate price range, with a payment plan it suddenly becomes affordable. (Have them sign a payment-plan agreement so it is all legal and aboveboard.)

## 4. Speak!

A study showing what is most important to clients when hiring someone revealed that 99.3 percent of the people pick the person based on the perceived image of quality. Well, that stands to reason. Image is everything—how you present yourself, your business cards, your web site, and so forth. You need ways to demonstrate your quality. As we've discussed, one of the best ways is speaking engagements.

Brush up your speaking skills. Speaking at local events is a sure-fire way to establish credibility and gain exposure. If this idea makes you cringe, join a public-speaking group so you can learn to speak confidently. Consider doing a joint seminar with somebody in a complementary business. You can share expenses, and if they have more experience than you, you can let them do most of the talking while still presenting yourself as an expert on stage with them.

Aim to speak at events that are related to your niche. This is where you will find your ideal clients. (Lions, Rotary, etc., are a starting point, but you need to aim for speaking engagements that are more specifically aligned with your ideal coaching clients.)

Speaking engagements also offer you the opportunity to sell products, books, and so forth at the back of the room. You can enroll people in your seminars, sell your products, and establish yourself as a credible expert who has the answers to their problems. You can prepare handouts that explain your services and expertise and encourage them to contact you. If you have a brochure, include this in your handout.

### Seminar Promotion Tips

Before you do a seminar, think about the topics that would most interest people. The title must also show the benefit. Find a location that is part of a credible business, like renting a room at a bank or the library. When you are trying to establish yourself, your seminars are going to be *free*. The goal is to get a lot of people to attend and then to convert those people to become clients.

You will need a leave-behind or handout that is geared to sell people on your products and services. *Not* an educational pamphlet or brochure, but a real *sales* brochure. You can also consider offering *gift certificates* for a service such as a free assessment or short consult.

In order to fill the room, you will place *ads in the local papers*, and you can also place preprinted announcements if your local paper accepts inserts. You should start to promote two weeks before the date of the seminar. Run the ad for two weeks in the Sunday papers prior to the event as well as the two days prior. You can also consider asking local businesses to post a notice on their office bulletin boards.

*The purpose of these seminars is lead generation.* To amp up this strategy and get more folks in the room and more leads, you can also:

- Rent a highly targeted direct-mail list (through a list broker) or from another professional with the same target audience. You want a list of prospects that have shown some interest in a similar service or use similar products.
- If you use direct mail, send the flyer twice. This pulls much better results. Mail four weeks prior then again two weeks prior to the event.
- Monday or Tuesday evenings get the best attendance rates.
- In your ad and flyer, use a testimonial and tell them what they will learn. Give them a free gift, too.
- Sell books, tapes, and other products at the back of the room.
- If you can find a trade organization, college, organization, club, or nonprofit to sponsor you, you will get more recognition and a credibility boost.
- So, get started by picking a date, making sure you don't schedule during a major holiday or sports event.

## 5. All Things Advertising

Spend your money wisely. Don't keep trying the same ad in different media if it was a flop the first time. Realize that if the ad didn't work the first time, chances are it won't work the next time. Something is wrong with it, and why would you waste your money repeating a dud?

Small businesses have neither the time nor funds to wage an image-advertising campaign; leave these techniques to the corporate giants such as Coca-Cola and Pepsi. You can run general ads that will promote your business and put it in the public eye, but as a tool for attracting your ideal client quickly, it is not effective.

What *is* effective is a technique called *direct-response marketing.* This technique serves two useful purposes: It targets your ideal client and requires them to take some form of action *now*, such as buy something, make contact for more information, make a donation, or some other form of action. It also provides statistical information to enable you to know which ad format works best, which form of media, and so forth because you have the response rate to gauge this. This enables you to tweak and hone your ad until it works perfectly. You can also grow your database by collecting (with their permission) e-mail addresses, phone numbers, and so on. No more wasted dollars on advertising that doesn't work and an easy way to grow your list!

To work, you must really know who your target audience is. This is not something you waste on the public at large. If you are a health-and-fitness coach, you'd be more interested in placing your ad in a health-and-fitness magazine as opposed to a magazine on stamp collecting or a general woman's magazine. Place your ad where your ideal clients are likely to read it.

Don't waste a brilliant direct-response campaign on something ordinary and everyday. Your offer must be extraordinary, and you have to use a headline that grabs their attention and makes them want to read the rest; don't use your name or business name as the headline. For example, if somebody is looking for a hypnotist to help them quit smoking, which of these ad headlines do you think is most likely to attract their attention?

**1.** Joe Blogs, Hypnotist.

or

**2.** QUIT That BAD HABIT or Your Second Treatment is FREE.

What you say in your ad is equally important. Readers do not care about you. They care about themselves. Don't waste your precious ad space talking about how clever you are or how many years you've been in business. Tell them what you can do for them, what problems you can solve for them, how you can help them. It must all be about *them*.

Don't include your prices up front. Your offering really might be the best on the planet, but your price may turn off people. Give them a chance to learn more and really understand how using your services will change their lives before you discuss price. Have them contact you for pricing information.

Make sure you take advantage of your efforts by keeping statistics. Take note of the response rate. Test your ad—it's headline, opening lines, the body, and, yes, even your pricing—everything. Tweak and retest. Eventually you will have an ad that is perfect for your business and will bring in the clients every time!

## *Winning Newspaper Ads*

Newspaper advertising is one of the best ways to promote your business. Many small businesses skip this form of promotion and miss out on a great opportunity. Before you can advertise, you must decide what product or service you want to promote. What in your business are the types of services that most people call for? Then you are ready to write powerful copy. Great copy is a combination of having a great headline and a visual that supports the headline. They combine a one-two punch and attract attention.

Think of your ad as a billboard. If the *headline and graphic* don't stop people, it won't get read. Using questions or starting your headline with "How to" produces the best results. Here are some sample headlines that work:

- Is your job making your life miserable?
- How to shine at interviews and land the job!

Now for the *body* of the ad. Most people don't really know why they need your products or services. So your ad copy must tell them what problem you solve. If they have that problem, then they are motivated to contact you.

A great way to write ad copy is to give a checklist of the things that are symptoms of the problem. Some examples:

- Do you feel tired?
- Do you have less motivation?
- Are you constantly feeling anxious about your weight?
- Do you have frequent headaches?
- Are you having trouble sleeping?
- Do you dislike exercise?
- Do you feel you've tried every diet program and nothing works?
- Do you get a lot of colds and flus?

Following the checklist, say why they should choose you to solve their problem. Give at least three to five reasons. Each reason needs proof. So if you say "excellent service," you can then say: 24–7 support line. Or if you say, "weight loss that stays off," give an example: Mary Smith lost 11 pounds 5 years ago and keeps it off with ease.

The next step is your *call to action.* You want them to take action *now.* People tend to put things off or forget, so you want to give them an offer that has them going to the phone or your web site *right now.* Include a deadline.

### How Much Information Is Too Much Information?

Use your web site or marketing materials, such as brochures, business cards, flyers, and so forth, to attract clients. Do provide information on what you can do for them, and on your web site you can include your background experience and qualifications.

Do *not* mention how many years you've been in business if you have just started. Nobody wants a new coach; they don't want to be *your* guinea pig! Play it down and emphasize past experience, if relevant, to support your current professional standards.

Do *not* show your fees up front on your web site or on your promotional materials. The reason being that many people are scared off by seeing large fees in print before they have a chance to really assess the value and what they will get out of it. Convince them first of your value to them, and then you can discuss fees.

Don't make the beginner's mistake of acting like you have lots of room for new clients, that you are just starting off, and have loads of free time. This hardly instills confidence! Get yourself a virtual assistant and have them set up appointments and liaise with your clients; it presents a more professional image and means you have better things to do with your time. (You can barter with some virtual assistants if you cannot afford one immediately.) If you can't afford a virtual assistant to begin with, use voice mail. Don't always answer the phone if you're doing nothing; let it go to voice mail because it gives the impression you are busy.

If some clever person asks, "How many clients do you have?" You can laughingly ask them, "Why, is that important to you?" If they are trying to ascertain how much experience you have, talk about your overall experience, not the number of clients you have and not how many years, months, or weeks you've worked as a coach. You have other appropriate life experience, no doubt, that can be counted quite honestly as your experience. Don't feel awkward about this, if you are being honest.

If newcomers in any profession were never given a chance, our professions would die out. We all know that suitably qualified coaches, even newbies, have a great deal to offer, and it is unfair to think they should not practice in their chosen profession simply because they are new. Of course, you never want to lie outright to anybody. There is never any excuse for deceit in this or any other profession.

### *Make Your Sales Letter Sell!*

Whether used on your web site, as an e-mailing, or as a direct mailing, your sales letter must be compelling and not just full of hype and oft-used blurbs. You have limited time and space to get your point across; you must keep their attention or you'll have wasted more than money. Your opening paragraph must be powerful and convince them to continue reading. Be direct. Use strong, actionable words that establish trust and credibility, but don't be pushy or manipulative. Offer something free, like a report or downloadable e-book, if they respond by a specified date. Your sales letter must make them take action *now* and give a response.

In your sales letter, tell them about yourself: name, business, background, why other people hire you, what you can do for *them*, and, perhaps, offer something free, like a special report. Reassure them that you are not trying to sell something.

Use the P.S. system. In your P.S., offer testimonials from previous satisfied customers or offer your free report. If you're stuck about ideas for free reports, why not come up with a top-10 list: The Top 10 Ways to Achieve . . . (whatever your coaching niche objective is).

If you suspect your letter isn't working, make one change at a time and test it before making further changes. You don't need to throw the baby out with the bathwater! Special reports are typically three to six pages long. You can take your top-10 list and build a paragraph around each point and easily fill three to six pages.

Next, to whom do you send this? Building your contact list is a priority. Use your own address book and local business papers and journals. You can buy specific lists from certain agents who will give you a list of your niche market in a specific type of business, but make sure you don't e-mail this list without their prior permission! This can be hard to establish, and with the new antispam laws, you can't afford to take risks. A flyer or physical letter may stand a better chance of being read than an e-mail that, if not deleted outright, may be caught in a spam filter and still not be read.

Market first to your target audience in your geographic area— within driving distance. You will appreciate this when you are required to attend meetings, conduct seminars, or give demonstrations. If you are not sure what mailing would be the most attractive, study the mailings you receive in your mailbox. What grabs your attention?

Visit the web sites of successful businesses and marketers and review their sales-letter copy. If you still don't feel confident writing your own, you can hire an expert to do it for you. This is Joe Vitale's area of expertise! Start by checking out his web sites. If you are going to hire a copywriter and you can't currently afford Joe, then shop around. You can also hire copywriters through http://www.elance.com, where the experts bid on your project. Realize that doing it this way is also a case of "buyer beware."

## 6. Convert Window Shoppers into Customers

Use lead-in products to convert window shoppers, such as web surfers, into customers. You use these products to enable you to meet clients with different spending power. It also works like Baskin-Robbins' little pink spoon, which enables your clients to get a taste of what's offered.

Lead-in products can be things like e-books, audio tapes, tele-classes, workshops, seminars, and even online e-courses. Inexpensive but attractive. If you don't have products of your own yet, sell products created by other people. If you become an affiliate of their programs, you can earn handsome commissions from every sale made on your web site. Passive income! And you know we're all for that, right?

You can also sell your lead-in products at speaking engagements. In fact, people are more likely to buy something at your speaking engagement than they are via your web site.

Focus your promotions on your cheaper lead-in products and services first. Get the clients in before you try to entice them to try your more expensive ranges. *Do* market these lead-in products to your target audience, and have a plan that will enable marketing to them on an ongoing basis, introducing them to the next step, which is your more exclusive, more expensive range of products and services.

## 7. Learn Sales and Marketing

Take responsibility for your marketing. It will save you a great deal of money. Learn the sales and marketing process. You can hire sales and marketing experts to do this for you, but realize it comes at a cost. If you can afford it, fine; if not, you'd better learn how to do it yourself.

Marketing is not a once-off project. It must be done regularly and consistently in order to achieve results, so it makes sense to learn how to do it yourself. There are many programs available to teach you the basics and the more advanced methods. You can attend live seminars or use study-from-home kits, audios, and books. (Check out http://www.TerriLevine.com, where you will find a variety of courses and materials to help you and that suit most budgets.)

If you can't afford to learn immediately and you can't afford an expert to do this for you, do some research on the web. Read the free articles and how-tos that you will find on many marketing expert's web sites. There is no excuse for saying "I don't know how."

## 8. Getting Free Public Relations

Contact local clubs, charities, and service organizations (like school bands, the Boy Scouts, Optimist Clubs, etc.) and offer to create for them *donation-dollar certificates.* Send them a *mailing* and also do a *follow-up call.*

The mailing will say that you have donation dollars to give them and want to participate with them in raising funds for their organization. When an organization sells anything to raise money (like Girl Scout Cookies), you will give donation dollars to each purchaser.

I tell them that I want to assist local charities in their fund drives and will give a donation dollar for something like a short coaching session, a free book, special report, and so forth. Some of those I have coached give away free consults, screenings, and assessments.

If they agree, I have coupons created that say "Donation Dollar for You" and then something like "Free Book." Then I include a short statement on the coupon:

Because you were generous enough to support a local charity [I keep the phrasing generic so I can use it for all charities and don't have to reprint], you've earned a free book.
Redeemable by calling: 877-401-6165.

Then I have my photo and my credentials and a short statement of what I do. And to drum up more of this free PR, I also add: "Terri Levine supports a wide variety of community organizations. She might be able to help you with your next fund-raiser. Call her for information."

Also include an *expiration date* to get them to take action now. Don't forget to send a press release to your local papers telling about this program and each time you are involved in a fund-raising activity.

### *Use Press Releases*

What I love about PR is that it works better than an ad because people don't trust ads but do trust what the media or other people have to say about you. Get a list of all your local TV and radio stations and newspapers. Think of something newsworthy or all the interesting things in your field and jot them down: statistics, something in your field, a client story, a little known fact, and so forth. Pick one to do your release about. Write a release answering who, what, why, where, and when in the first paragraph *without* selling anything. Tell how this information affects people in your industry or clients who use your industry. Include the name of your town at least twice. No jargon. Go back and add a powerful title on the release that includes your town's name. Send an action photo of *you* doing something related to the story. Send it to your newspapers and TV and radio stations. Call to see if they received it, want to do a story on it, or interview you or have you on to talk.

Another idea is to read publications about your industry and the types of clients you work with. Every time you see a remark you agree or disagree with, send a press release to your *local* publications and radio and TV stations either supporting or refuting their remarks. Be sure to tie this into your *local* community's concerns.

### Spread Your Fame

If you have been on TV, in newspapers, or on radio, you can leverage the exposure. Send postcards to your database telling them about the show. After you have been on, send a brief note saying if they missed it, you will send them the tape or a transcript. Same with the newspaper or magazines; send them the clipping.

You don't need a PR firm to land you a radio interview. Contact radio stations yourself. Send them an information package about you, and tell them how you can help their listeners. There are also many stations that broadcast their shows via the web. Do a web search and you will find those that resonate with your line of business. They are always looking for new guests to interview. Don't be shy!

Think about hosting a community or client-appreciation event. This is a great way to reach new prospects and reactivate old ones. Because we want to get you free PR for great exposure, tie the event to a cause.

For example, you can get a free coaching session *if* you bring in a toy for tots or can of food for the homeless or send a donation to the American Cancer Society. You not only show the public you care, you also have a great reason to contact the press. In most cases, they also will send crews to cover the event if you do this out of an office. Call local radio and cable TV stations and ask if they would let the public know about this as a free service.

At the event, chat with people and try to set up time to speak with them for about five minutes after the event for the purpose of telling them about your service and seeing if they might want to be a client.

## 9. What to Do When You Need Clients Fast!

Desperate? You want clients fast and you have little money to spend? Here are some other ideas you can employ:

- Ask other professionals who have similar clientele (e.g., career coach and resume writer or speech pathologist and pediatrician) to put your literature in their offices, and offer to do the same for them. Include a coupon for a free service. The idea is you send business each other's way.
- Go where your target audience is (Borders, Starbucks, a gym, etc.) and, using your letterhead, place a half-page letter and a

half-page coupon under windshield wipers of the cars in the parking lots.

- Go to nearby offices and drop off the flyers, asking the receptionist to give one to each employee.
- Look into a Valpak coupon book. It's inexpensive and reaches a huge audience.
- Remember the weakest form of communication is e-mail. Next weakest is snail mail. And the number-one strongest form of communication is in person—by more than 500 percent! Get out there and see people. Hand out your new practice brochure.
- Offer a price reduction to create fast income. Create a mailer, ad, flyer, and co-op coupon about this.
- Mail to your database often, and send coupons with expiration dates for services.
- Ask for referrals. (Create a frequent-referrer program.)
- Ask a successful associate to endorse you to their clients and give them a percentage of your sales. (Create your affiliate program!)
- Promote when you are busy. Never stop. Never, ever, ever quit!

## 10. Other Forms of Self-Promotion

People want to hire somebody who is obviously doing it better than they are. So everything about you and your business must display success. Review all your business cards, brochures, letterheads, and any other business documents you use, including your own appearance. Review your web site. And don't look only at appearances; include things like how you handle client queries, how you answer the phone. Ensure all your contractors, virtual assistants, and other staff members are well versed in your quality-assurance procedures.

### *Use Credentials*

Credentials go with credibility and trust in the mind of the public. They might not even know what the initials behind your name stand for, but they like to see them. Credentials impress. In reality, the person without the initials may be much better qualified and provide a better service, but the public doesn't know this. So, put things like your degree abbreviations and any certifications after your name. The more, the merrier.

### Make Your Business Cards Sell for You

Business cards are *not* business expenses; they are ads that generate money if you use them right. Your business card must tell what you do and why they should hire *you*. Remember, differentiation! This requires a maximum of one or two lines of copy. Some samples:

- Pain-free dentistry.
- Design at half the cost.
- Coaching in your home.

In addition, your card needs a graphic. The purpose of the graphic is to get the card, which is your *ad*, noticed and read. Be sure the graphic conveys a proper image and nothing boring, dull, or inappropriate. Graphics expand the copy and enhance it.

Your card should not look *too* expensive, or people will be intimidated. It should not be run off from a computer and look too cheap, either. It should be something in the middle.

I personally prefer a fold-over card so you have three sides on which to put copy and graphics. Be sure the typeface is clean and easy to read. Use color combinations that are bright and lively. A smartly designed business card tells more than how to contact you. Make your business card work for you. Graphics, logo, word choice.

### The Right Brochure

Fact: Most companies in business, no matter what size, have a brochure or sales literature. Its purpose it to create more credibility and sales for your business.

Keeping in mind that a brochure has the purpose of selling, why do most brochures end up in the circular file? To me, it seems because they are dull and boring and have a similar look and feel. This creates disinterest and leads to a person not spending time to read the brochure.

A brochure backs up your credibility and promotes further repetition of who you are and what you do. It gives you material to leave behind or distribute when you give talks or attend fairs. You can leave them on your doctor's reception desk or anywhere that *your* potential clients might see it.

## Why Most Brochures Don't Work

The first rule about brochures is if the copy doesn't help make a sale, it doesn't belong there. Brochures are not places to educate or inform. They are sales tools only. So, prices, hours, and such *don't* go there. The purpose of the brochure is to convince people and sell them but not educate and inform them. It must answer the question about what your business does and then give them reasons to choose your business over all others. In addition, it should establish a feeling of trust and your credibility as an expert. If you remember that your brochure's intent is to get people to take action and contact you and nothing else, you will create a great brochure.

Once you've created a great brochure, don't let it become just another business expense. It must become a business *asset*. In addition to placing your brochure in strategic places, you can use it for:

- Whenever you have a phone or web contact or any inquiry who does not become a client, send them your brochure.
- When someone sets up an appointment to meet or speak with you, send them your brochure. This serves to firm up the appointment, resell them, and take away any reasons they have for not keeping the appointment.
- When you meet with someone in person or right after their first session, give or send your brochure along with your curriculum vitae to convince them you are the expert.
- Use your brochure to get clients to refer. Give them copies to give to friends, coworkers, family, and so forth.
- Whenever you give talks, your brochure is your leave-behind.

And, whenever you want to get booked for talks and they ask you to send them something, send your brochure along with your outline for the talk.

## Reactivate Old Clients

Clients with whom you haven't been in contact for years, and maybe even left under not quite the right circumstances, often flow back after a small tickle.

Create a letter telling them why it is beneficial for them to come back as a client right *now* and what may happen if they don't. I recommend putting in a special offer as well. You can also reactivate by using the telephone.

You may wonder why bother with a former client who has not responded to your offerings. It is because people are busy, business is busy, and there are multiple priorities and messages. They may still need and desire your services.

Write a one- or two-page letter. Be sure to tell them why it is important that they return to your services *now*. Add a special or deal. Mark on the outside of the envelope "Address Correction Requested" so you can keep your database clean. Mail first. Then phone those who don't respond to the mailing.

### *Frequent-Referrer Programs*

I continue to be amazed, after being in business for more than two decades, that most people do not ask for referrals. It is the most successful marketing strategy on the planet, yet people aren't asking. I think it is because they aren't comfortable and don't know what to say.

All you have to do is *ask!* If you don't ask people to refer, they won't, and you'll waste money, energy, and time marketing to find clients. To get an even better response to referrals, I created a program many years ago that is highly successful and that I teach to business people. The strategy is based on the principle that if people feel good about referring, they will refer more people.

I deeply appreciate and acknowledge client referrals. I call people and thank them. I write them a thank-you note, and I send them a thank-you gift. You should consider establishing a gift program. For the first referral, I recommend a gift that is priced between $5 and $10. Pick items they will want to display in their offices or homes. Also, inscribe the gift with something like, "Deep thanks, Comprehensive Coaching U." Some of the gifts I have sent over the years include an acrylic clock, a calculator, and a paperweight.

For the second referral, follow the same system and send a more expensive gift worth about $15 to $20, such as a notepad with calculator (engraved again), an emergency car kit, or a thermos. For extra referrals, I work in increments of three. For each third referral, I bump the gift's value. So, it might be lunch at their favorite restaurant, a weekend getaway, and so forth.

## Set Up an Affiliate Program

I also have established a program for affiliates who are happy to promote my services and products because they earn generous and worthwhile commissions. These people are doing your marketing for you, and you can reach thousands of people you'd otherwise have to pay high advertising fees to reach. The commissions you pay out are well worth it.

Educate your existing client base about the other services and products you offer. To be sure your current clients know *all* you provide, send them a package by mail. Send this to all clients you ever had. Make this look like an important letter, and on the envelope write "Address Correction Requested" (because you also want to keep your database up to date!).

The first sentence must be powerful to intrigue them to read the entire letter. People buy products and services because they solve a problem. What problem do they need to have solved? What new product or service do you provide or have more information about? By providing this key information, you will also gain referrals from this database because you are once again positioned as the credible expert.

After you spend time solving a problem for them, which is your opening paragraph or two, then tell them what is new in your business. This is when you describe new products and services; also include testimonials and other endorsements. Again, you are the expert.

If you have been on a radio show, been in print, spoken at an event, and so forth, tell them about it. Tell them to call with questions or to download a free report or how to make an appointment with you.

Add a P.S. telling them to refer people who need your services and products and that most people don't know your products and services are available, so they can really serve their friends, family members, and coworkers. Offer a free assessment, tool, and brief consult so their friends can learn firsthand what you do. Include three gift certificates they can give to those they know. And then, follow up. One mailing is a start; three or four work best. So change the letter slightly and mail it out a few times.

Marketing your business can be as cheap or as expensive as your budget and time allow. But now you know you can do it yourself, even on a limited budget.

# 17

# Putting It All Together

*Vision without action is merely a dream. Action without vision just passes the time. Vision with action can change the world.*

—Joel Barker

By now you should be feeling that, yes, it is possible for you to market your own project or business. So now here's one more little tip that will help you make the most money in the quickest time.

Using the Google search engine again, find out what this week's most popular searches have been. This will tell you what topics are hottest at the moment. Pick one of these hot topics and prepare an e-report or an e-book related to that hot topic. Put it up on your web site and start marketing it. Ask affiliates to promote it, too. List one copy of it on eBay as well, and that's all you have to do.

It works like this:

1. First, go to http://www.google.com/press/zeitgeist.html and see what the most recent popular searches are. You're looking for the latest, hottest topics.
2. Pick one that interests you.
3. Now do some research. You can use the Internet for this, too. Compile as much information as you can about this hot topic. This material is going to become your special e-report or e-book. Don't plagiarize; use your own words. If you need or want to copy something verbatim, get the original author's permission first. Your aim here is to develop a product on

a subject about which people are currently searching the Internet. You're going to give it to them in one handy e-book! (You can create an e-book as a Microsoft Word document and convert it to a PDF file, but if you want help to create great e-books, try http://www.7dayebook.com.)

4. Now you create a one-page web site. You need only one page for this; it's the page where you are going to market and sell your new product. You can put up sites at http://www.godaddy.com (a one-page site there is only $14.95 per year). Or use http://www.citymax.com/?domain=239124&door=5&referral.

5. Now list one copy of your product on eBay. The purpose of doing this is to get your product and site noticed right away by millions of people the world over.

You now have a product about what people are currently interested in and will, therefore, buy. Not convinced? Read on.

Have you seen that book about the movie *The Passion of the Christ*? It is nothing but questions and answers about the movie. Truly! All the book consists of is compiled data, and yet it became a best seller. Why? Because it tied in to the immense interest in that movie; people wanted to know more about it. The book was a hit, and the author found himself on national TV and radio shows.

You really can do this, too. How easy is it? You don't even have to wrack your brain to come up with a topic that will sell. Just search Google. Then create something that ties in to one of the popular searches, and you're on your way.

For example, if you do a search and discover one of the top searches this month happens to be creative uses for navel fluff, you can do some extra research on the subject, find an interesting angle to it, and produce an e-book called *100 Creative Uses for Belly-Button Fluff*.

All you have to do to put everything together is take action now. It's never too late, if you start *now*.

There are a million ideas just like this one that can help you create a rewarding, exciting, and lucrative coaching business. The only thing that can hold you back from becoming a successful coach is your own mind. If you're still hearing the self-doubt, finding difficulties in staying motivated and focused, aren't getting the support you need from others, or aren't putting all these ideas into practice, read this book again. And check out the free gifts and discounts and all the resources in the back of the book to further help you become a successful coach.

Watch out for self-defeating tendencies, follow the formulas and ideas we've outlined, and just do it!

# Recommended Resources

## Coaching Resources

Comprehensive Coaching U

http://www.ComprehensiveCoachingU.com
A one-stop shop for all your coaching needs and resources, including links to all Terri Levine's other web sites and resources.

The Coaching Institute

http://www.coachinstitute.com
Coach training information and resources.

TLC: TerriLevine.com

http://www.terrilevine.com
Personal coaching, programs and courses, articles, books, tapes, DVDs, videos, and other educational and training resources for personal and business development and improvement.

Coaching Kits (coach training by home study)

http://www.terrilevine.com/kits.htm
The following kits are available for home study:
    Deluxe Comprehensive Coaching Kit
    Basic Comprehensive Coaching Kit
    Selling without Selling Kit
    Attract High Paying Clients That Love You Package

Basic Stop Managing Start Coaching Kit
Deluxe Stop Managing Start Coaching Kit
Work Yourself Happy Kit
Magnetizing Money System

The Comprehensive Coaching U Success Library

http://www.comprehensivecoachingu.com/success-library.htm
For existing coaches and those interested in becoming a coach, "the
leading success strategies and tactics have been assembled on one
place so that you can immediately think, coach, and market just like
world-leading coaches." Discover all the tools and systems you need
to easily and quickly grow your coaching practice.

Selling-Without-Selling Kit (for home study)

http://www.comprehensivecoachingu.com/SellingWithoutSellingKit
.htm
For sales professionals, sales managers, sales teams, and entrepreneurs.

Comprehensive Coaching U BrainSpeak Program

http://www.comprehensivecoachingu.com/brainspeak.htm
The Comprehensive Coaching U BrainSpeak system is an advanced
tool of consciousness that is designed to expand the brain and mind
by increasing brain-wave activity and synchronizing both right and
left hemispheres. This transformational audio series can support you
in achieving growth and change.

The Coaching Success Profit Generator

http://www.terrilevine.com/software.htm

http://www.coachsuccesssoftware.com
The Coaching Success Profit Generator is the ultimate coaching success software. It's a comprehensive system that contains easy and
fun-to-use generators, analyzers, and modules guaranteed to help
you create or improve your coaching business as soon as you start
using it.

Dozens of Free Marketing Resources

http://www.pascoaching.com/free_resources.htm

Find free articles, reports, and tips along with referrals and discounts for printing marketing materials, e-mail marketing, and publicity.

Assessment as a Unique and Effective Marketing Tool

http://www.CoachingAssessments.com
Assessments draw prospects to your web site and convert prospects to clients. These low-cost assessments created by Larina Kase and Milana Leshinsky will help you market your coaching business and improve the quality of your coaching.

Coaching Business Action Plans

http://www.CoachingBusinessPlans.com
You know how important a business plan is in planning and achieving your business goals. But you don't have the time, energy, or interest to write one. You don't need to when you use these information- and idea-packed plans.

Dr. Joe Vitale's Executive Mentoring Program

http://www.joe-vitale-executive-mentoring.com/info.html
For in-depth coaching in marketing.

## Other Coaching Resources

Solution Box (David Wood)

http://www.life-coaching-resource.com/

http://www.solutionbox.com/
Products for establishing a coaching practice, solutions for coaches.

Business Building Center (Stephen Fairley)

http://www.BusinessBuildingCenter.com

Coachville

http://www.coachville.com
The coaching school that started it all; coach training, listings, and resources.

Life Coaching Web Site Design

http://www.lifecoachwebsolutions.com/

Web site design specific to the coaching industry.

24–7 Coaching.com

http://www.247coaching.com
Coaching directory, class locator, programs, and resources for the
   United States and United Kingdom.

Peer Resources (Canada based)

http://www.peer.ca/coach.html
Programs, listings, and news; coach training and professional
   development.

College of Executive Coaching

http://www.executivecoachcollege.com
The leader in coach training for professionals with graduate
   degrees.

Career Coach Institute (Marcia Bench)

http://www.careercoachinstitute.com/
Specific career coach niche training.

Find a Coach

http://www.coachinstitute.com/findacoach.htm
Listing of qualified trained professional coaches for personal
   coaching and mentorship.

Find a Life Coach

http://www.findyourcoach.com/
Coach listings and resources.

Coaching from Spirit

http://www.coachingfromspirit.com
Specific spiritual certified coach training and spiritual coaching
   resources and programs.

International Coach Federation

http://www.coachfederation.com/eweb/
Certifying body initially set up by Thomas Leonard (Coach U) to
   certify his own students, now open to other coaching associations.

Coaching Association of Canada

http://www.coach.ca/

Find a Life Coach U.K.

http://www.findalifecoach.co.uk/
A U.K./European life-coaching directory.

Association of Coaching and Consulting Professionals on the web

http://www.accpow.com
An all-in-one resource for motivated coaching entrepreneurs.

PR Web

http://www.prweb.com
Free place to list and distribute press releases.

Annie Jennings PR Publicity Superstore

http://www.anniejenningspr.com/publicity-superstore.htm
Need PR resources? Annie Jennings PR Publicity Superstore is a
  publicity hub that's packed with powerful CDs and digital recordings that teach you how to be a publicity pro!
Free Publicity CD Offer: Please get Annie's free publicity CD "The
  Only Secret to Getting Booked on Oprah: The Rest Is Strategy"
  at http://www.anniejenningspr.com/only-secret-to-getting-on-
  oprah.htm.

## Books

Auerbach, J.E. (2001). *Personal and executive coaching: The complete
  guide for mental health professionals.* Pismo Beach, CA: Executive
  College Press.

Auerbach, J.E. (2005). *Seeing the light: What organizations need to know
  about executive coaching: The 2005 state of the coaching industry report.*
  Pismo Beach, CA: Executive College Press.

Beck, A.T. (1976). *Cognitive therapy and the emotional disorders.* New
  York: Penguin Books.

Coach U. (2005). *Coach U's essential coaching tools: Your complete practice resource.* New York: Wiley.

Fairley, S. (2003). *Getting started in personal and executive coaching.* New York: Wiley.

Fairley, S.G., & Stout, C.E. (2004). *Getting started in personal and executive coaching.* Hoboken, NJ: Wiley.

Kase, L. (2005). *The successful therapist: Your guide to building the career you've always wanted.* New York: Wiley.

Kase, L. (2006). *Anxious nine to five: How to beat worry, stop second guessing yourself, and work with confidence.* Oakland, CA: Harbinger Publications.

Levine, T. (2000). *Work yourself happy.* Buckingham, PA: Lahaska Press.

Levine, T. (2001). *Coaching for an extraordinary life.* Buckingham, PA: Lahaska Press.

Levine, T. (2003). *Stop managing, start coaching.* North Wales, PA: CCU Press.

Miller, W.R., & Rollnick, S. (2003). *Motivational interviewing: Preparing people for change* (2nd ed.). New York: Guilford Press.

Vitale, J. (2005). *The attractor factor: 5 easy steps for creating wealth (or anything else) from the inside out.* New York: Wiley.

Vitale, J. (2006). *Life's missing instruction manual: The guidebook you didn't get at birth.* New York: Wiley.

Vitale, J., & Mok, J.H. (2005). *The e-code: 33 Internet superstars reveal 43 ways to make money online almost instantly—using only email.* New York: Wiley.

Williams, P. (2004). *Total life coaching: 50+ life lessons, skills, and techniques to enhance your practice . . . and your life.* New York: Norton.

## Articles

Prochaska, J.O., & DiClemente, C.C. (1982). Transtheoretical therapy toward a more integrative model of change. *Psychotherapy: Theory, Research and Practice, 19(3),* 276–287.

Sherman, S., & Freas, A. (2004,November 01). *Harvard Business Review,* 82–90.

# Gifts to Help You Become a Successful Coach

## One Free Gift and Two Bonus Offerings for You, with Compliments of Terri Levine

To redeem any or all of these offerings, please visit this page on Terri's web site: http://www.terrilevine.com/successful_coach_d_b.html.

1. **Free gift.** Nine-week Marketing Strategies to Build Your Business to Its Full Potential E-Course (valued at $599).

   This e-course is designed for anyone who owns a business—no matter what size—and works for service- or product-based businesses. You will receive nine special e-mail lessons, one each week for nine weeks, on nine specific topics.

   These powerful strategies are worth thousands of dollars in revenue and will save you thousands in wasted marketing time and money, including information on how to keep your clients, get repeat business, and generate referrals all in one step. Put simply, you will get to learn the secrets of how Terri Levine markets and how her clients do it and you will learn to do it, too.

2. **Special price (just for you) on Terri's Attract High Paying Clients package.** Normally priced at $299, Terri is offering to you for only $100 plus shipping (and tax if you live in Pennsylvania).

This package contains all the information provided from two special-event teleclasses taught only once by Terri Levine: Attracting High Paying Clients and the Advanced Techniques to Attract High Paying Clients Courses.

The Attract High Paying Clients package includes the following: eight hours of audio cassette tapes from the eight-week How to Attract High Paying Clients That Love You teleclass. Plus for a limited time we're including—for free—two e-manuals (regularly priced $200) with enhanced materials developed based on the classes, not a transcript of the calls.

3. **Special price (just for you) on three months' membership to Terri's Success Library.** Regularly priced at $99 per month with a one-time membership fee of $50, Terri is offering you three months' membership for only $9.00 per month—no other fees.

    When your special three months' membership expires, you can choose to cancel or to continue; we can arrange recurring billing (at the regular rate) until you say stop.

    This Success Library is the ultimate turnkey coaching practice system. All the leading success strategies and tactics have been assembled in one place so that you can immediately think, coach, and market just like world-leading coaches. Every three months, you will receive a power-packed set of leading coaching products to help you turbocharge your success. The Success Library tools and systems represent a total value of more than $8,000. You get all these for your small monthly membership fee.

## Two Free Gifts and One Special Discount for You, with Compliments of Larina Kase

To redeem, contact Larina through the web site http://www.PAScoaching.com. State which gift you would like, and be sure to say that you have *The Successful Coach*.

1. **Free gift.** The e-book *From Therapist to Coach* for mental health professionals transitioning to coaching.
2. **Free gift.** A package of three articles on secrets to making marketing successful e-mailed to you.

3. **Special discount (just for you) on the telegroup Mastering Marketing for Coaches.** This is a small group led by Larina with up to eight coaches who are serious about building their businesses. You'll benefit from the energy and ideas of the group as you receive highly customized coaching and consultation at a fraction of the price of individual coaching. You'll receive a bonus of $100 off the group and many free resources, such as copies of effective letters to referral partners and proposals for projects and joint ventures.

## Gifts for You, with Compliments of Joe Vitale

1. **A free marketing course by e-mail.**
   Simply send a blank e-mail to class@aweber.com and you'll get "Recession-Proof Marketing," a seven-part training series by Joe Vitale.
2. **Dr. Joe Vitale's main web site contains dozens of free articles on marketing.**
   http://www.mrfire.com

# Index